T0072380

DIALOGUE

HOW TO HAVE DIFFICULT CONVERSATIONS

IGNITES

ABOUT RACE, GENDER, AND VIOLENCE

CHANGE

JOY RICH

BALBOA.PRESS
A DIVISION OF HAY HOUSE

Balboa Press books may be ordered through booksellers or by contacting:

Balboa Press
A Division of Hay House
1663 Liberty Drive
Bloomington, IN 47403
www.balboapress.com
844-682-1282

Print information available on the last page.

ISBN: 979-8-7652-4196-7 (sc)
ISBN: 979-8-7652-4197-4 (e)

Library of Congress Control Number: 2023908517

Balboa Press rev. date: 05/09/2023

This book is dedicated to humanity.

This Book Belongs to:

____

CONTENTS

INTRODUCTION

If you have ever wanted to have a conversation about a difficult issue but just didn't know where to begin, this book is for you. The premise behind writing this book is to equip you with all the skills needed to engage in difficult conversations. Let's face it, life is complex and therefore full of complicated matters. Since we are aware of this, we should prepare to deal with tough issues when they arise; which they inevitably will.

Throughout this book, I will be coaching you on the fundamentals of difficult conversations. I have curated seventeen concepts that will teach you the necessary framework for engaging in difficult conversations. The seventeen concepts are: self-awareness, self-regulation, self-determination, asking questions, effective listening, reflective statements, internal locus of control, separating individuals from the issue, reframing, perception, positivity, humor, the Pygmalion effect, win/win outcomes, future-focused thinking, big picture outlook, and relaxation. These concepts are drawn from my background in mediation and management.

Furthermore, the seventeen concepts lay the foundation for the CALM Dialogue construct. The CALM Dialogue is a four-step process that I created to enable anyone to engage in tough conversations. Since the seventeen concepts lay the groundwork for the CALM Dialogue, you must learn them before embarking on using the CALM Dialogue. This is because they will give you the knowledge that is necessary for using the CALM Dialogue process effectively.

Additionally, this book is filled with personal stories from real life examples. The names of individuals have been changed to protect their identities, but the stories are all true. All the stories in this book were chosen to enrich the content, and breathe life into the content and concepts that may otherwise be too complex and boring to grasp.

As well, this book is filled with games and exercises to keep you engaged and your mind stimulated. Games are a great way to make learning new concepts and ideas fun. So, make sure you take your time and enjoy the journey of learning the ideas by completing each chapters' activities.

The answers to the games are located at the end of each chapter for quick reference.

There are also sample dialogue scenarios about race, gender, and violence for you to go through. These behavior reproduction exercises will allow you to see how the CALM Dialogue is used to tackle tough issues. As well, you can also create your own scenarios by using the templates in the Appendix section at the back of the book. This will allow you to build confidence while engaging in dialogical practice about issues you may want to address in your life. My hope is that you will use this book to help you transform and improve your relationships, your community, and your world.

HOW TO USE THIS BOOK

I recommend that you read this book from the beginning to the end. Don't skip over chapters. This is because each chapter builds on the previous chapter. Therefore, you should read one chapter at a time. Once you have finished reading a chapter, you should then complete the exercises and games at the end of the chapter. This will allow you to fully digest the content. The games and exercises are a way for you to engage with the material, so that you can absorb it. Once you have finished learning the material from one chapter, you can move on to the next chapter. Ideally, if you read and work through one chapter a day, you may be able to retain the concepts better.

I want you to take ownership of this book. Write your name in it. Underline in it. Highlight in it. Fully embrace this book. The more you use it, the more fun you will have with its content. So, what are you waiting for? Grab a pencil and get started!

CHAPTER 1

Conversation Illuminates the Future

"If you want to be a voice of peace in the
world, begin by making peace
a permanent condition of your own life."
-Wayne Dyer

The Awakening

There's nothing like the sound of a ringing bell to snap you back to reality. Grief filled the air as I sat there in what would be one of many ceremonies required to be performed as part of a Hindu death ritual. My grandfather had passed away three days prior. My cousin had called me to inform me of the news. I quickly scrambled to get plane tickets from Utah to Toronto for my daughter, husband, and myself. It had been a whirlwind. The funeral was held two days after he had passed away.

This particular day was the day after the funeral. It was the day I was finally able to catch my breath. As an attendee at a Hindu ceremony, it was customary to sit on the white sheets that covered the floor and listen to the pandit speak. His talk that day was about the Bhagwat Gita. I remember him saying that the entire book was about internal conflict.

Hold up, wait a minute! What? As I leaned forward and cleaned the cobwebs out of my ears, a light bulb suddenly lit up in my brain. So, one of the oldest texts ever written is all about internal conflict. Holy cow!

I felt like this was vital information. Why was that not information that was told at more of these religious gatherings? In fact, this information needs to be common knowledge for all regardless of religious affiliations. Maybe, this information would be able to help people if they were aware of the fact that everyone had internal conflict.

The first thing I did when I returned home was order my copy of the Bhagwat Gita. Thanks to my Amazon Prime membership, I was able to get my hands on it quickly. After devouring its contents and allowing myself time to digest it; I was able to understand the timeless message. I discovered that the epic war that was fought in the Bhagwat Gita could be interpreted as being fought in the battlefield of the mind. I was blown away by this realization.

I felt like Neo in *The Matrix* after he had taken the red pill. My eyes were opened to the Universal truth. We are all in the grip of some kind of internal or external conflict. It is a fact of our collective consciousness. It is woven into the DNA of our very existence.

The reason this message resonated with me may have been because previous to this awakening, I was a mediator and had written a few booklets on a conflict resolution process that I had created; the CALM Dialogue. The CALM Dialogue is a simple 4-step method that could be used by anyone to resolve disputes. It provides individuals with a quick set of tools to put in their toolbox to use when they are faced with disputes. I had also taught a class on the concept at the local University via their Continuing Education Department. The student feedback that I received from the participants was great and encouraged me to want to continue to develop my concepts further. I then created an online course on a Learning Platform where I have had thousands of people take my course and learn about conflict management.

I have since realized that the 4-step CALM Dialogue process could also be used to have difficult conversations in general. Now, I want to teach everyone the CALM Dialogue so that they may incorporate it in to their daily lives. My intention is to help individuals via conversational coaching in order for them to be able to better deal with disputes. If internal and external conflict is faced by all, then everyone should know how to deal with it. In fact, everyone should anticipate that conflict will occur and be prepared to deal with it through the art of conversation.

Why Discuss Difficult Issues

The main reason people should discuss difficult issues is because the world is a complex place. Difficulties can be found at home, school, and in the workplace. For me, the quote by Benjamin Franklin, "In this world nothing can be said to be certain, except death and taxes," should be changed or amended to say, "In this world nothing can be said to be certain, except death and conflict". That rings true for me and a lot of people that I know all over the world.

In recent years the conflict in society has increased exponentially. The world has been plagued with the Covid pandemic; which has raised issues of health care inequality. Racial tensions are elevated; which has raised awareness of the unequal treatment of minorities. As well, tensions have also increased in homes all around the world due to the increased number of remote jobs. So, the need for skills to handle disputes is almost a necessity at this point.

The quote that is found at the beginning of this chapter is key to unlocking conflict resolution for all. As Wayne Dyer said, "If you want to be a voice of peace in the world, begin by making peace a permanent condition of your own life." But how? Well, that is where this book comes in handy. The objective of this book is to assist you in acquiring the necessary understanding and techniques that you can utilize when dealing with the difficult issues in your life.

Apparently, many people do not know how to have difficult conversations. That's according to the authors of the textbook on *Adult Learning*. As stated by Merriam and Bierema (2014) "It has been our experience that learners do not often know how to have a conversation with someone with whom they disagree, so helping learners build competence in this area while working with challenging concepts is fundamental to the critical thinking process" (p. 232). Just to be clear, I consider anyone that has a pulse to be a student of life or a learner, so you are included in this broad description. This book will try to rectify the issue of people not being able to converse with those who have differing opinions by providing a process that will allow anyone to quickly learn how to maneuver and engage in difficult conversations. In today's society, there are plenty of difficult conversations to be had on subjects such as race, gender, and violence.

There are also people who may want to achieve other goals and objectives other than resolving a conflict. There may be people who want to work on ways to prevent a dispute from escalating. Some people may simply want to improve their competency in managing conflict. Others may want to strengthen their communication skills for engaging in difficult conversations. Whatever your objective is, you will need to learn the foundational concepts that lead up to the CALM Dialogue construct.

The CALM Dialogue will be covered in detail in chapter 7. However, you will need to learn some key concepts before you dive into using the

4-step process. Without a full understanding of why and how you would use each step, the process may not be used effectively. It is like driving a car in a foreign country where you don't speak the language. You may know the steps required to drive the car; however, without understanding what the road signs mean, you will not know how to effectively navigate your way to your desired destination.

Years ago, when I lived in the Bahamas, my friend Cora from Canada came to visit me. One day I was driving her around when she blurted out, "I feel like we're in India! Everyone keeps honking their horns and yelling out their windows while driving on the wrong side of the road." (Full disclosure, she was of East Indian descent.) I just laughed because I had forgotten that I was driving on the left side of the road and using my horn to let someone over or to thank someone for letting me over all while using a round-a-bout to get to the other side of town. All of these foreign driving techniques had become second nature to me. So, just like anyone can learn to drive in a foreign country, I believe anyone can learn how to have difficult conversations. Therefore, by the time you have finished reading this book, it is my aim that conflict management will become second nature to you.

Critical thinking is a core component when it comes to conflict management. Some may wonder why they should engage in critical thinking when it comes to dealing with conflict. Well, for one thing you will be able to better assess your beliefs, actions, and assumptions through a critical lens. As well, you will be able to challenge and test your own thinking and mental capabilities. A key element in critical thinking is self-correction. Therefore, if you start to realize that there are things that you may need to work on, then that is a step in the right direction.

As none of us are perfect, there is room for improvement in all of us. A long time ago, I was part of a church group that met weekly. One evening we were discussing ways that we could become better versions of ourselves. During the discussion, one of the participants named John, stated that he was already a good person and did not need to improve. The priest looked at him and said, "Then the only thing left for you to do is to give away all of your worldly possessions and go live among the poor." The look on John's face was priceless. So, the moral of the story is: we can all improve ourselves, in one way or another.

As I mentioned earlier, I teach about conflict and I was a state certified mediator. So, throughout this book, I will be introducing mediation concepts that pair well with dispute resolution techniques as part of my conversational coaching method. The co-mingling of the two will allow you to gain further insight into dispute management.

One tactic that is used in mediation is the concept of focusing on the future. Mediation encourages participants to look at what would help them move forward in their lives. This is the first concept you will utilize on your quest to having constructive conversations about difficult issues. I believe that people should strive towards being future focused and not past centered when resolving or managing conflict. One important thing to consider is that conversational coaching is not therapy. The main objective of coaching will be to get you to understand how you can best manage difficult issues when they arise. Just think of it like a remote with a broken rewind button. The only buttons that work on the conversational coaching remote are pause, play, and fast forward.

Race, Gender, Violence

Throughout this book I will discuss race, gender, and violence. As I have first-hand experience with all three subject matters. Firstly, I am of south Asian descent. My ancestors left India in the early 19th century and settled in Guyana; a small South American country. When I was six years old, I moved to Canada and spent my youth there. In my twenties, I then moved to the Bahamas for 5 years. Now, I reside in America. So, I have been an immigrant in three different countries and have lived among various races.

Secondly, as a woman, I have experienced discrimination in the workplace and within the family structure. I know firsthand that females in most Asian families receive different treatment from their male counterparts; as the society is a patriarchal one. I have also experienced sexual harassment in numerous workplace settings.

Thirdly, violence is something I have witnessed personally. I have been the target of violence at school, in a work setting, and in the home. I have also witnessed violence. I do not condone violence in any way. In my opinion, the best weapon to use against violence is speech.

It is my belief that dialogue can ignite change when it comes to race, gender, and violence. It is my desire that the knowledge and skills obtained through this book will lead to a more peaceful and understanding world. For we create our reality with our thoughts, actions, and words.

When I was asked to teach the CALM Dialogue at the University along with my views on how to use it to resolve issues pertaining to race, gender, violence, and religion; I was surprised to say the least. This was primarily because my class proposal only outlined teaching about my 4-step CALM Dialogue process. The only way that anyone would have known that I proposed using it to tackle tough issues like race, gender, violence, and religion was if they had gone online and researched my training material. At first it seemed like a daunting task to be able to tackle such complex issues in one class. But it worked. I was able to demonstrate how the CALM Dialogue could be used to deal with complex issues.

For the purposes of this book, I have decided to just touch upon race, gender, and violence. This is because I believe that they are the most prevalent issues that plague our society today. They seem to be at the very core of all the conflicts that permeate the soundwaves of media. As well, these three topics are something I can offer personal insight in to; as opposed to being an outsider looking in.

When I was pregnant with my daughter, I went to the doctors for a checkup. That particular day a medical student was there. He was asking me questions. One of which was did I have any cramping. I wasn't sure what he meant so I asked him to describe what it felt like. He then responded, "How am I supposed to know?" In that moment I realized that he was not able to relate to me or any other pregnant woman that came in for a check-up. So, the point of this story is to let you know that I will only talk about what I can personally relate to in this book.

The main reason that I devised the CALM Dialogue was because when I was studying leadership, I realized that conflict was prevalent in almost all workplaces. Management spent a lot of their time dealing with disputes on a regular basis. I had learned that people needed processes to deal with their issues and not just theories. I then decided that this was good advice for everyone both young and old. Children needed processes just as much as adults did. So, I wanted to create something that was simple enough for a child to understand, yet complex enough to deal with adult issues. The CALM Dialogue was formulated to deal with conflict at home, school, and work. As well as tackle issues of race, gender, and violence.

It has been my observation that violence is often intertwined with gender and race. There was a shooting at a business in 2021 where the victims that were targeted were Asian females. The innocent victims lost their lives because of their race and gender. Two things that were inherently bestowed upon them. So, by simply being who they were created to be, they were victimized and killed. Hopefully, the perpetrator can get the help he needs. If only he had been able to manage his anger and had learned how to deal with conflict constructively; maybe those lives would have been spared.

One of the most memorable days I have stored in my memory bank is the day I became an American citizen. The day I was sworn in just happened to be April Fool's Day. At the time I was residing in Charleston, SC. There were four of us undergoing the Naturalization process that day and none of us had any family members in attendance. Tears filled my eyes as we watched the videos and listened to the speeches of what it meant to be an American citizen. I remember how proud I felt that day as I relished in the fact that I would now be able to enjoy countless freedoms that other people in different countries only dreamed about.

That memory flashed before my eyes as I watched in utter disbelief as the Capital Building in Washington, DC was stormed by rioters in 2021. My jaw dropped as I absorbed the images on the television of people breaking windows and pushing their way into the building. Some protestors had weapons while others had restraints. There were some taking selfies while chaos was unfolding around them. It was a scene right out of the movies. I could not believe the violence that had come over those individuals. These were American citizens. They are all supposed to be overjoyed because they live in a country that is filled with freedoms and rights.

The storming of the Capital Building illustrates that people can be influenced to act in irrational ways. However, I believe that if people can be influenced to commit vile acts that damage society; then maybe they can be influenced to act in ways that foster the betterment of society. So, I applaud you for wanting to learn more about having difficult conversations pertaining to race, violence, and gender.

The Importance of Conversation

The name of this chapter is Conversation Illuminates the Future. Over the past few years, we have all heard "let's have a conversation about the tough issues." However, some people do not know how to broach the subjects of race, gender, and violence. They are often at a loss for words. That is why it is important to learn how to have a conversation about topics that are difficult. Once we can do this, we will be able to have a brighter future for humanity.

Conversational skills are paramount to tackling issues and breaking down barriers. One day Eli—a teacher that I know—told me about an incident that occurred at her school. A student named Hudson asked an Asian teacher—Miss Patel—if all East Indian people smelled. She then went on to say that the Miss Patel was so stunned by the question that she did not know what to say. I was surprised that a teacher could not summon the words to dispel such a hideous stereotype. To me it was clear that a simple conversation using the CALM Dialogue could have resolved the issue. If Miss Patel was able to articulate an answer, then it would have squashed the stereotype that Hudson was curious about. That was a teachable moment that was lost due to a lack of conflict management skills by Miss Patel. When used effectively, conversation can be utilized to shed insight into complex issues.

Like any skill that you want to develop, dialogical skills need to be used in order to develop. One needs to engage in conversation about difficult topics to hone their skills. Only through the use of words can we as people continue to evolve. So, I truly do believe that conversation will illuminate the future.

We as human beings all need to look deep within and see how we can create change for the better. As Gandhi said "Be the change you wish to see in the world." That change that we all long for starts with each of us. Individually, we must all strive to do better, so that collectively we can all be better.

There is an ancient proverb that speaks about where the Gods hid wisdom. They wanted to place wisdom where it could not be easily found. They discussed at length where to hide this treasure. They talked about burying it deep under the ocean. However, they decided that people would eventually dive into the ocean and find it. They discussed hiding it on the top of the highest mountains. However, they decided that people would eventually climb the mountain and obtain the knowledge. Then they discussed hiding it deep within the person. They agreed that this would be the best place to hide wisdom; for people would never think to look within themselves to find it. Therefore, if you take the time to look within, you will be able to uncover the attributes that you possess that will enable you to have difficult conversations. Once these gems are honed and polished; you would have found your hidden treasure.

Exercise 1

Circle all the phrases that you think apply to you.

I am a people pleaser	I do not need to please others
I am a good listener	I do not listen to others well
I talk over others	I give others the opportunity to speak
I see things the way others see things	I see things differently from others
I am empathetic	I do not feel empathy for others
I am aware of things that bother me	I am not aware of things that bother me
I think before I speak	I say the first thing that comes to mind
I take charge of my life	I let life happen

Exercise 2

Visualize ***what you look like*** when you are faced with conflict. You can draw a picture in the box if you want or you can simply visualize it in your mind's eye.

Exercise 3

Visualize ***what you want to look like*** when you are faced with conflict. You can draw a picture in the box if you want or you can simply visualize it in your mind's eye.

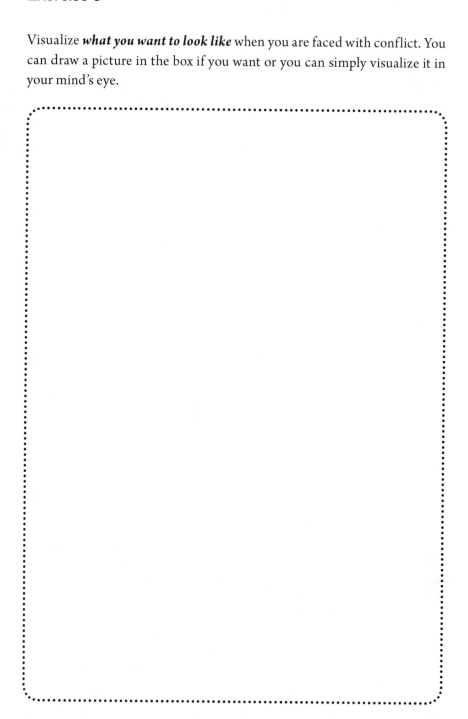

Chapter 1 Word Search

```
M A C G E N T P M A O B C S S C H K L C
A S O R A T T A B U O G F A B O Y N O O
T T N A E E T S O M I L N U I N I M Y L
E A F C T T L I D T E N V E T V M W O E
P T L E I B W I B I W T E N D U I O T P
N W I U E S L R A R I W R D N R R T S I
O R C B G E N D E R N P S I V S T E T N
I S T A T E S E N T W A C R H A E I A D
T Z O A N C T E A T I A L A M V N R P I
A X G S T A S K M E T T O C U I I R Y V
S C U G K F E R H I A A R H H O S O M I
R V E H I D F T O H L X U P L L T L E D
E B K L K E F N E T E B E I J E E N N U
V N T K Y M I R R O R X R C I N R O T A
N M Y P E R C E P T I O N E C C B V K L
O A T D S T Y T E M E N T S I E W O R P
C E N O I S S U C S I D I A B O G U E S
A F R T E D I S S U E N L I G T E N H U
```

Words To Find			
CONVERSATION	DISCUSSION	COMMUNICATION	FUTURE
RACE	GENDER	VIOLENCE	

Chapter 1 Pangram

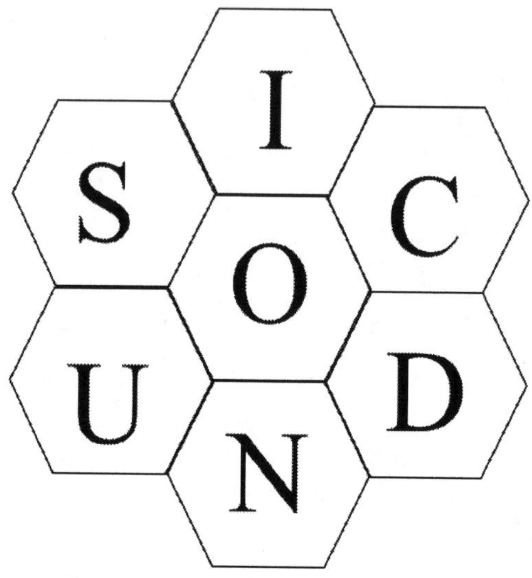

Use all the letters in the pangram to create a word from chapter 1. You can use letters multiple times. Write the word you made below.

Chapter 1 Word Scramble

Unscramble the following words.

Scrambled Word	Unscrambled Word
notionversca	
cussdionis	
mutaionicomcn	
ecar	
rendeg	
turfue	
evenclio	

Answers

Chapter 1 Word Search Answers

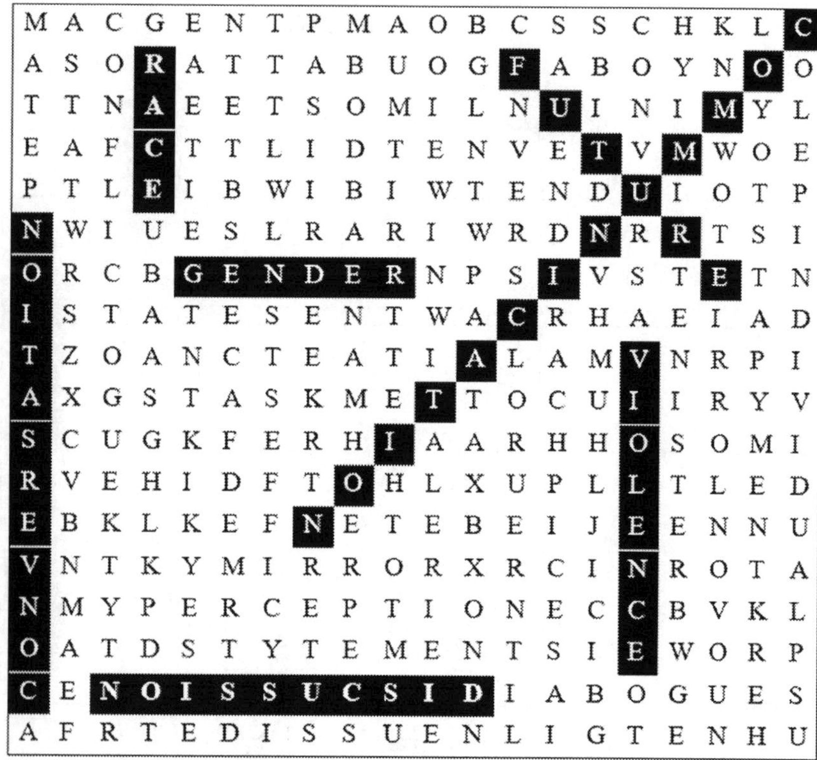

Chapter 1 Pangram Answer

Discussion

Chapter 1 Word Scramble Answers

Unscrambled Word
conversation
discussion
communication
race
gender
future
violence

CHAPTER 2

Fan the Embers of Empathy

"You cannot always control what goes on outside.
But you can always control what goes on inside."
-Wayne Dyer

Empathy

Imagine a hot, sunny day filled with the scent of lavender blooms, as a little girl dressed in blue bops up and down in anticipation of a cold treat. She is beaming with delight as she waits with her mother by an ice cream stand. Her father smiles and hands her a pink, mouthwatering, three-scoop ice cream cone. She squeals with excitement. Just as she leans over to taste it the three pink orbs fall to the ground. She lets out a shriek as tears roll down her face.

Most would be able to empathize with the little girl. It would be easy for the majority of people to feel her disappointment and understand her pain-filled tears. As adults, many of us have experienced disappointments and can relate to the dismay felt by the little girl. This is because we can access memories of pain that we have stored in our minds from our own previous disappointments.

Empathy is a feeling that almost all of us have had at one time or another. Empathy is the ability to relate to others. It is based on your ability to put yourself in another person's situation and sense their emotions. Essentially, it is your ability to walk in another person's shoes. Empathy is without a doubt the ultimate people skill.

It has been my experience that empathy cannot be bought or sold; it must be learned. There is no store that will sell it to you. There's no price you can pay to acquire it. One must learn it through experiences or exercises. Therefore, it is my hope that by the end of this chapter you will have improved your empathy skills.

Now, have you ever heard of the term "emotional intelligence"? Well, it was coined by psychologist Daniel Goleman. The concept of emotional intelligence encompasses five competencies; self-awareness, self-regulation, motivation, social skills, and empathy (Adler, 2008, p. 170). Individuals who are emotionally intelligent are able to handle social situations effectively. As well, emotionally intelligent individuals possess better people skills than individuals who are not emotionally intelligent.

Did you know that some animals exhibit empathy? Dogs are known to show signs of empathy when their owners cry. Elephants are known to bury their dead. They cover the carcasses with branches to hide the bodies of the deceased. If these animals can show signs of empathizing for other beings, then surely most people are capable of improving their empathy skills.

Developing one's empathy skills will definitely pay off in the long run, especially when it comes to dealing with tough conversations. So, how can one improve their empathy skills? Well, you can start by paying more attention to a person's facial expressions, body language, and speech patterns when they are speaking to you. By doing this, you will be able to pick up on cues that will tell you how the person speaking to you is feeling. I find this to be helpful with face-to-face conversations. For instance, when someone is texting you, the tone of the message is often lost. That's why I prefer to talk to people on the phone and then whenever possible face-to-face to further develop my empathy and communication skills.

My earliest memory of feeling empathy was when I was in primary school. Mrs. Ali—a teacher—had come to work covered in bruises. I remember her crying and telling the other teachers about her ordeal. Mrs. Ali told them that her husband had gotten drunk and abused her. I recall the sadness I felt for her. Unfortunately, even though I was very young, I had witnessed domestic violence and was able to comprehend her pain on some miniscule level. I knew that when someone got beaten, it made them feel sad. So, I felt sad too.

Have you ever noticed that babies are great at expressing themselves? When they are hungry, they cry. When they are sad, they cry. When they need attention, they cry. People always seem to be able to relate to the needs of a crying baby. This may be due to the fact that babies are small and innocent. Using this logic, if you want to become more empathetic, start paying more attention to the small children that are around you. In no time, you will quickly notice that there will be plenty of opportunities to hone your empathy skills. This is because kids are always falling down and scraping their knees. They may on occasion break their favorite toy. As well, kids are always getting sick with colds and coughs. I find that being around children helps you develop empathy for the simple things in life. This is a good way to start out, because then you can work on your empathy for more complex issues.

Most Guyanese people will tell you that mosquitos are quite prevalent in Guyana. Since I was born in Guyana and lived there for the first six years of my life, I was used to having to deal with the itching and scratching that accompanied the bites. However, when I moved to Canada, most Canadians did not really encounter mosquitos on a regular basis. In fact, mosquitos were only spotted during the short Canadian summers. According to a dermatologist that I saw, I didn't have lily white skin, therefore, I was susceptible to keloid scarring. So, when I itched my bites, it resulted in my skin getting scarred.

My mosquito allergy was received with a lack of empathy on a regular basis, from people I knew. People that I encountered would talk about the dark marks I had on my legs. It made me feel ashamed and disgusted with myself. Family, friends, and strangers alike, all seemed to unite when it came to teasing and belittling me. No one seemed to care or feel any empathy for me. I felt completely alone. I would often cry and wonder why I had to be afflicted with this ailment, when others didn't even have an itch when they got bitten by a mosquito. Why was my reaction so severe, while others had no reaction at all?

Years later, I was visiting a relative in Canada. She had invited a few of my cousins over as well. My cousin, Amy, called me over to show me my cousin Maya's legs. Amy pointed and said, "Look at Maya's legs! Aren't they gross?" As I looked at Maya's legs, I recognized the black circles that dotted her skin. I immediately knew that she too was afflicted with the same mosquito allergy that I had. In that moment, a wave of empathy washed over me. I just stood there frozen, as if in suspended animation, for what seemed to be eternity. My past hurt resurfaced and bathed me in a shower of emotion. Finally, fighting back tears I managed to utter, "Maybe you could try using bug repellant. It really works for me."

After that interaction, I knew why I was plagued with the mosquito allergy all those years ago. It was so that I could develop empathy for others who may be afflicted with skin ailments of their own. Due to my personal experience battling my own dermatological issues, I am able to really feel for and understand the suffering that people who are plagued with skin ailments encounter. In hindsight, I can see now that my mosquito allergy was one of my greatest empathy teachers.

Another story that comes to mind about empathy is when I had just arrived in Canada. I was six years old. I had never been around people from various races before. Even though Guyana has a diverse population; I only lived among people of Indian descent. So, when I moved to Canada and started attending a school that was primarily composed of Caucasian students, it was a culture shock. I remember being called names like "Paki". At that time, the racial slur was lost on me due to my lack of geographic knowledge. I later found out that the term was meant to describe an individual from Pakistan. The slur was used to belittle anyone that had brown skin. Whenever I heard it, I knew that people were trying to intimidate and insult me. It made me feel scared and small. I heard it all the time, so I was scared and intimidated a lot. The slur was even spray-painted on a few overpasses so even if you were not able to hear it, you were always able to see it. As a child, I couldn't comprehend why people were so mean and hateful towards me. I often wondered why I was brown. I also wondered why I was not born white, like what seemed to be everyone else. I hated my skin; I hated myself.

Years later, I was working at a clothing store in a mall in Canada. I usually worked part-time after school and on weekends as a sales associate. One evening, a mother came in with her daughter that was about six years old. They came to the cash register to pay for the merchandise they had selected. I was ringing up their items when I heard, "Mommy, why are some people brown, and some people white?" I looked at her and smiled. Her embarrassed mother did not respond and quickly left the store after paying for her purchase. Instead of feeling anger toward the child, I felt empathy. After all, that was the very same question I had asked myself years ago when I was six years old. Once again, I found myself realizing that my skin was one of my greatest empathy teachers.

The Wayne Dyer quote at the beginning of this chapter, "You cannot always control what goes on outside. But you can always control what goes on inside," is quite fitting in regards to empathy. This is because when you truly relate to someone, you are controlling what is going on inside of yourself. You cannot control what others do and say, but you are able to control your response and reaction to what is happening around you. Once you are able to put yourself in their position and feel their emotions, you will be able to relate and connect to them on a more meaningful level.

If you are not as empathetic as you would like to be, you can always improve your empathy skills. As well, if you are empathetic and want to further develop your empathy, you can. One way to do this is by watching movies. Since that's something we all do anyways, why not brush up on your empathy skills and be entertained at the same time? So, fill your empathy basket by viewing some movies that are known to be emotional or tear jerkers. If you are a dog lover, you would enjoy watching *Marly and Me* and *A Dog's Purpose.* I remember watching *A Dog's Purpose* at the theater. By the end of the movie, there wasn't a dry eye in the theater. It was an emotional and empathy filled cinematic experience. Hallmark commercials are also good at eliciting emotional responses, especially around Christmas time. There are many places you can access videos and stories. All you have to do is actively start to seek out footage that will help you to further develop your empathy muscles. When you have good empathy skills, you will be able to communicate more effectively with others.

Effective Listening

Have you ever heard of the stoic philosopher Zeno? Well, thousands of years ago, he famously said to one of his students, "We have two ears and one mouth, so that we can listen twice as much as we speak." How brilliant! This quote still rings true today, even though it was uttered millennia ago. The wisdom in those words will live on forever as they are a universal truth.

When you listen effectively, you should embrace the concept of silence. Silence is also used as a mediation tactic. It is an important concept because it allows both parties to be heard. While you listen, you should restrain yourself from talking. Hence, you should not interrupt the person speaking. This is sometimes a difficult task for some. But with some practice, you can manage to stop interrupting others mid speech.

When my daughter was in kindergarten, they would always be encouraged to stay quiet when lining up, in order to better hear instructions.

On one such occasion, I heard her teacher say, "Put a bubble in your mouth and listen." The children's cheeks all puffed out as they put a bubble in their mouths and listened. I thought to myself; what a cute and effective way to get someone to listen and not talk.

So, the next time you find yourself starting to interrupt someone, just put a bubble in your mouth. You don't have to puff out your cheeks. Your bubble can be the size of a grape. Certainly, this is something anyone can learn to do if a kindergartener can do it.

One of the most important skills I learned as a teenager working in sales was how to listen. People assume that one learns how to sell as a sales associate. However, it has been my experience that selling a product is tied to listening to the customer. When you listen to the customer, you will find out what they actually need. Therefore, by effectively listening to a customer, you will help them to purchase what they want and need.

The store that I worked at as a teenager was a store for older women. So, it wasn't cool or trendy. The sales associates consisted of elderly women. I worked most closely with Rose, Iris, and Lilly. They were all very experienced in sales and customer service. Essentially, they became my listening mentors. As my mentors, I observed them closely and understood that they were more interested in building rapport with customers by taking the time to talk with and listen to each person. They were not obsessed with upselling customers with unnecessary products. By listening to the customers, they were able to gain customer loyalty. Of course, as a teenager I didn't realize that I was learning how to become an effective listener. I only realized years later that I learned to cultivate my listening skills while working with more experienced female mentors.

My retail adventure continued while I was in university. I managed to get a job as a sales associate at a store in the new city I had moved to. It was located in the downtown area of the city. Compared to the first store I had worked in, this store was a bit more on the trendy side. In fact, it catered to a much younger clientele. Even though I only worked a few evenings and weekends, I always had good sales. One day my manager, Luna, asked me, "How do you sell so many items?" At that time, I didn't know. So, I just smiled.

Since the store was part of a retail chain, it had a corporate head office. This meant that the corporate office kept track of the sales for all of the stores. Consequently, the corporate office would give each location a monthly sales quota that they had to achieve. The company would also keep a record of how much merchandise each sales associate sold. This was achieved through a reward program. The associates received a different color star based on how much inventory they sold. At the end of each week, stars would be pasted by associate's names on a chart located in the staff room. If you reached your goal, you would get a gold star beside your name.

Needless to say, I was receiving gold stars regularly. I didn't realize it at the time, but the skills that I had gained from my listening mentors had allowed me to exceed my sales goals. By listening effectively to the customers, I was able to give them what they needed. For instance, when customers asked me for my opinion on the size, color, and style of an item, I would answer them honestly. As well, I would emphasize that they should not get hung up on the sizes printed on the labels; as they changed every season. One season, a size 8 could be a size 6. Another season, a size 8 could be a size 10. Instead, I shifted their focus to how the item of clothing made them feel as opposed to having them focus on what size the label defined them as being. By truly listening to the customers and providing honest feedback, I gained their trust.

Incidentally, all the sales associates were required to wear the merchandise that the store was currently selling. The company would assist with the cost by giving associates store dollars based on their sales along with store discounts. Most of the sales associates wore a top that was being carried in the store at the time with a plain suit. Each season, they would simply buy some new tops and switch them out. According to them, they were just doing what the company required of them. However, being young and I guess naïve, I did the complete opposite without even knowing it. I would buy outfits from each season's collection. I would have skirts and tops, pants and blouses, dresses, earrings and bracelets. As a result of this, I tended to sell more of what I was wearing. Inadvertently, the more clothes I bought and wore in the store, the more clothes I sold. This was because I was showing the customers what they would look like in a particular outfit. In a way, I was the living example of "practice what you preach." If I was telling others to buy something, I had to first buy it myself. Once I bought the clothes and wore the clothes; I was able to sell the clothes.

Likewise, once you are able to buy into the concept of effective listening, you will be able to don it while speaking with others. You too will eventually start racking up gold stars for your listening skills. In fact, every time you stop yourself from interrupting someone by putting a bubble in your mouth; give yourself a gold star!

Empathetic Listening

Empathetic listening is the marriage between empathy and effective listening. In order to listen empathically, one must listen with empathy. Now that you have had some experience with the concept of empathy, you will be able to better understand the concept of empathetic listening. This is where you listen to the person that is speaking to fully understand what they are saying. Therefore, you would listen without thinking about what you are going to say next. You just simply listen with both of your ears.

My first job out of university was as a cost accountant. It was at a small metal manufacturing company. At first, I was so happy to be working there. Everyone seemed so nice. Prior to working there, I used to look forward to Fridays. Who didn't? Friday afternoons were officially the start of the weekend for me and everyone I knew. TGIF (Thank Goodness It's Friday) was a huge part of my vocabulary.

However, the first Friday that I worked at the metal company changed my view about Fridays. I was sitting at my desk punching numbers into my calculator and checking the time periodically as it was Friday afternoon. A staff meeting was taking place in the conference room. The head accountant, foreman, a few managers, and Joe—the owner of the company—were having their weekly staff meeting. I was in the middle of calculating the cost of a particular project. Suddenly, the bellowing of profanity came pouring out of the conference room. I remember being shocked and horrified. The swearing and yelling ensued for thirty minutes. I was unable to concentrate on anything. It had me in a state of disbelief. I couldn't believe the way Joe was yelling at his staff. The poor men.... They just sat there and endured the vile abuse. None of them spoke back. None of them defended themselves. None of them dared disobey. They were all too afraid of being fired. I felt sorrow and despair for them, as I sat there with my calculator.

Every Friday would be a repeat performance. I quickly began dreading the Friday staff meetings, as well as the day itself. Even though I was never part of the meeting, I always got a knot in the pit of my stomach because I would have to sit there and listen to the violent rage that bombarded my workspace for thirty minutes.

The strange thing about the situation was that Joe would never treat the three women who worked for him in the same manner. On the contrary, he felt no remorse about treating the men that worked for him like slaves. The fact that men didn't always get favorable treatment in the workplace was an eye-opening concept for me. This was because I had previously only encountered gender bias against women in the workplace. I decided then and there that all workers should be treated with respect, regardless of their gender.

One Friday, I went to work and started crying. I just couldn't endure the way the workers were being treated anymore. My empathy for them was just too great. I circled a date on my calendar and decided that I would either find another job by then or I would quit. Fortunately, I found another job and reclaimed my love of Fridays.

As I studied management years later, I realized that great leaders motivate their followers; they do not intimidate their followers. To truly become a great leader, I believe one must listen to the needs of their followers. If one doesn't listen to their followers; they will have no followers to lead. One way to listen empathetically is by asking questions. When one asks questions, one can better understand the situation. So, what kind of questions should you ask?

Open-ended questions are the best questions to ask someone when you are trying to gain understanding about a particular situation. An open-ended question is a question that can't be answered with a simple yes or no. It allows the speaker to have the opportunity to tell their narrative. An example of an open-ended question would be: "What do you like about your new home?" This allows the speaker to talk about their new home's interior, exterior, yard, neighbors, etc. Therefore, it will be up to the speaker to decide how much or how little information they wish to share.

One day, while working at the mall, I was the victim of workplace violence. My then boyfriend, Aiden, had been told that someone had seen me at a restaurant with two guys and a girl. Aiden had come to the mall to see me during my break. We were standing in a part of the mall that was not visible to a lot of people. I was trying to tell him that the friend I was with asked me to go with her to hang out with some people she knew. The only reason that I went with her was because she didn't want to go by herself. Aiden refused to listen to anything I had to say. In his mind, he had created a scenario of his own and didn't want to hear the truth. He refused to listen to me as he slapped and hit me. I managed to escape him and returned to work.

Upon entering the store, my co-worker gasped at the sight of me. My face was swollen and I was crying. She looked at me and asked, "What happened?" I quickly recounted the incident. She immediately picked up the phone and called mall security. They were able to apprehend Aiden and he was banned from the mall. I didn't press charges or call the police, because I just wanted to be free of him. I kept thinking to myself, "Why didn't he want to listen to what I had to say?"

During my ordeal with Aiden, my co-worker had asked me the open-ended question, "What happened?" This enabled me to tell her what happened in a manner that I felt was appropriate. She was empathetic in her listening because she understood the severity of the situation and quickly notified the appropriate people. They were then able to act accordingly and escort Aiden out of the mall.

Another technique that could be used in empathetic listening is a reflective statement. This is when after listening to a person speak; the listener paraphrases or restates the speaker's words out loud. By doing this, the speaker is able to agree or further clarify their message. A reflective statement also enables the listener to better understand the situation at hand.

The day after the workplace violence incident, I recounted the events to my friend, Angel. She listened to me with empathy and used reflective statements. After I told her the story, she said, "So, he didn't listen to anything you had to say and hit you." I agreed with her assessment by saying, "Yes, that's what happened." Angel then went on to tell me that if someone cares about you, they do not hit you or abuse you. She also told me that if he did it once, he was going to do it again.

As I sat there, I truly listened to Angel because she had listened empathetically to me. Her words resonated with me. Angel convinced me to walk away from that relationship. I believed that I would be better off without him because of her encouragement. Her listening gave me the strength I needed to shun Aiden. So, no matter how much he apologized; I didn't go back. No matter how much he cried; I didn't go back. No matter how much he called; I didn't go back. I knew that Angel was right. I also knew that she had my best interest at heart as she was able to really empathize and connect with me. My hope is that this story demonstrates how profoundly empathetic listening has impacted my life.

Looking back on this narrative, I now realize that I was able to break free from an abusive relationship, as well as from the cycle of domestic violence. Growing up in a culture that is filled with violence made me think that violence was acceptable. However, by having Angel—who was an outsider—tell me differently, was my saving grace. As Aiden was also Guyanese, he may have been taught that violence was acceptable. So, by not accepting his violence towards me he too may have realized that violence is not acceptable. In the end, we may have both learned a valuable lesson.

Remember that when you empathetically listen to someone, you may affect their life in an unexpected way. I am sure that when Angel gave me her words of wisdom, she didn't know the huge impact it would have on my life. Therefore, the next time you have the opportunity to listen to someone; jump on it. You might just change their life and earn yourself a gold star for listening.

Exercise 1

List the names of empathy-filled movies or videos ***you have watched***.

1.

2.

3.

4.

5.

6.

7.

8.

9.

10.

Exercise 2

List the names of empathy-filled movies you ***want to watch***.

1.

2.

3.

4.

5.

6.

7.

8.

9.

10.

Exercise 3

Visualize ***what you look like*** when you are empathetically listening to someone. You can draw a picture in the star if you want or you can simply visualize it in your mind's eye. This is the picture you could visualize every time you earn yourself a gold star for empathetically listening to someone.

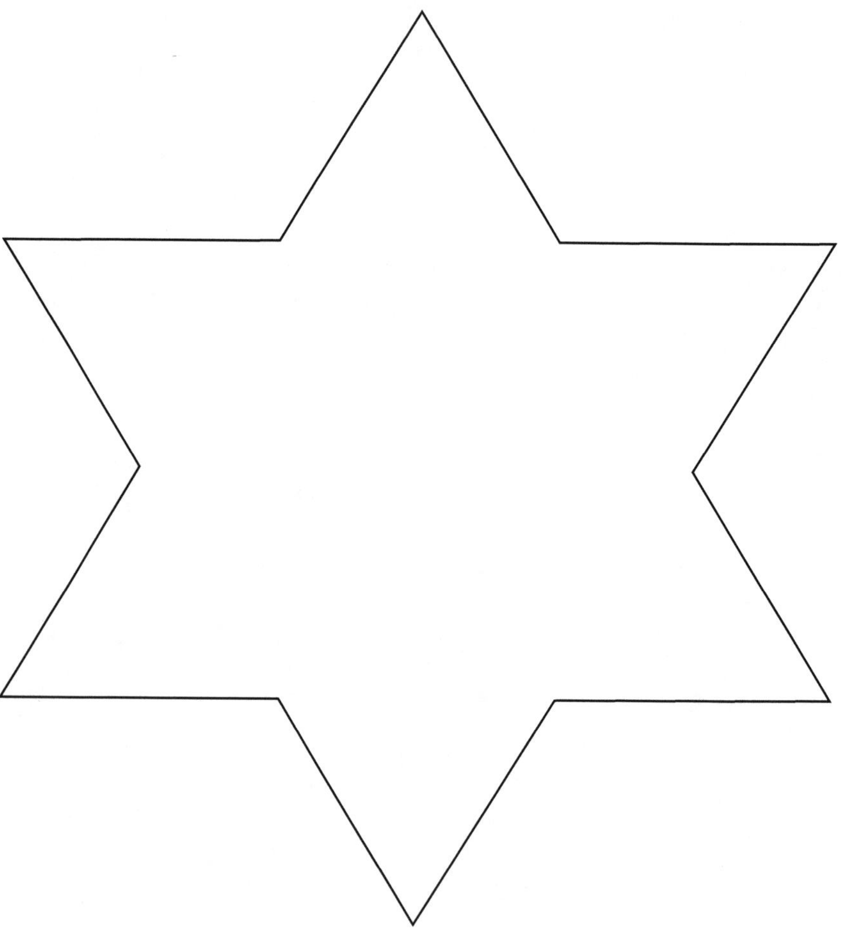

Chapter 2 Word Search

```
S T N E M E T A T S E V I T C E L F E R
E S O R A T T A B U O G O A Q O Y N W E
L T N U N D E R S T A N D U N G I E Y L
F A P T T T L I D T E N E E G V L W O F
D T L E I B W I B I W S E N D E G O T C
E W O U E S L R A R T W R D U R S T S O
T R C B A M I H V I N P S E V E T A T N
E S T A T E S E O F A W A R E M O I A T
R Z O A N C T N A T G R L A M P N R P R
D X G S T A S K M E N T O C U A I R Y O
E C U G K F E R H C I A R H H T S O M L
D V E H I D F T P H N X U P L H T L E D
N B K L K E F Y E T E B E I J Y E N N O
E N T K Y M I R R O T X R C I O R O T A
N M Y P A R C O P T S Y N E C N B V K T
E A T D S T Y T E V I T C E F F E O R P
P E L F H E G U Y A L M O N B O G U E S
O S E L F R E G U L A T I O N T E N H U
```

Words To Find		
EMPATHY	EFFECTIVE	LISTENING
QUESTIONS	OPEN ENDED	REFLECTIVE STATEMENTS

Chapter 2 Pangram

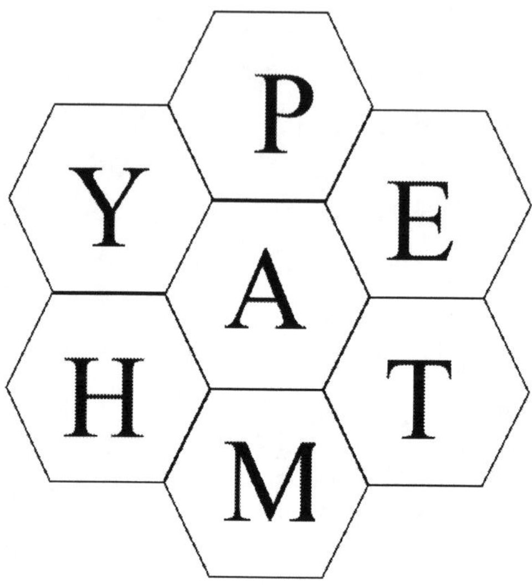

Use all the letters in the pangram to create a word from chapter 2. You can use letters multiple times. Write the word you made below.

____

Chapter 2 Word Scramble

Unscramble the following words.

Scrambled Word	Unscrambled Word
apetmhy	
fivetecfe	
itensling	
nopendeed	
nosestiqu	
livefetecr tentsmeats	

Answers

Chapter 2 Word Search Answers

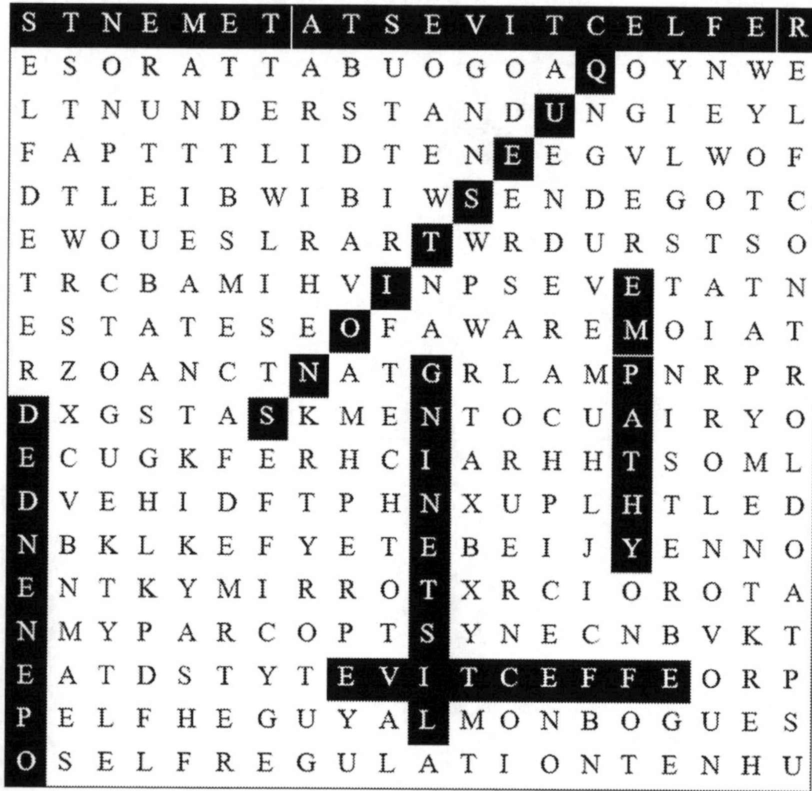

Chapter 2 Pangram Answer

Empathy

Chapter 2 Word Scramble Answers

Unscrambled Word
empathy
effective
listening
open ended
questions
reflective statements

CHAPTER 3

Set Your Vision Ablaze

"When you change the way you look at things,
the things you look at change."
-Wayne Dyer

Perception

Just thirty minutes prior, I had been in Divorce Court. The only thing I was able to walk away with was my freedom. I didn't receive any land, assets, or money. The only thing I was granted was the dissolution of my sham of a marriage.

I sat on one of the hard and uncomfortable chairs in the reception area of a Bahamian bank; waiting for my now ex-husband Vlad. The courtroom scene replayed in my mind as I recalled being the star in my own personal tragedy, which had unfolded before a live viewing audience. I didn't know what to expect at a divorce proceeding because I had never been to one before. So, to my dismay, I was shocked and embarrassed to find that the courtroom was filled with people. What made it worse was that I knew some of the individuals there. I felt my face turning red, and all I wanted was to have the floor below open up and swallow me whole. Due to the fact that I don't live in a graphic novel, that didn't happen. Instead, I had to stand there and endure the proceedings.

As I answered the judge's questions, I cried and my voice was shaky. At one point the judge shook his head and sighed, as if he didn't want to give me the divorce. I silently prayed that he would grant it quickly so I could disappear. Eventually, I heard the sound of his gavel as he ruled in favor of the divorce. I shed a few more tears, but they were no longer tears of sorrow, they had somehow been transformed into tears of joy. For I knew that I was finally free to begin again; free to be happy again; free to be me again.

The hearing probably only lasted for twenty minutes. However, they were some of the longest minutes of my existence. They say that time flies when you're having fun. So, I can only assume that the opposite must also be true. Time must slow to a grinding halt when you are having a painful and mentally excruciating experience.

Vlad eventually emerged from the private banking offices holding a white envelope. He looked at me and said, "I'm glad that you didn't decide to come after me for half of my money." Vlad then handed me the envelope that contained enough money to get me a ticket off the island. As I boarded my plane, the only things I possessed were my suitcase stuffed with clothes, two degrees, and my freedom. For me, that was enough, because my freedom was everything and it was priceless.

On the other hand, Vlad relished in the thought that he had gotten off scot-free because he didn't have to give me any of his money. He was beaming with pride as he thought he was the smartest person to have ever lived because he was able to get away with all of his money. The whole ordeal demonstrated that he was a master manipulator and a dedicated liar. Even though we were together for more than a decade and all the assets belonged to both of us, he made sure that everything was in his name. But that was fine, because I was content with my freedom.

However, the Universe has a way of leveling the playing field. Years later, Vlad was prosecuted by the SEC (Securities and Exchange Commission) and was found guilty of securities fraud. As a result of the ruling, he would no longer be able to work in the financial industry. Furthermore, he was also slapped with a $30 million fine.

Based on your perception, who do you think is better off? I perceived my freedom as priceless. Whereas Vlad perceived his financial earnings to be the ticket to his freedom. But now, he has a debt to pay and a score to settle. His actions caused him the very thing he valued the most—his money. On the contrary, I have the ability to travel freely, live peacefully, and sleep soundly. Based on my perception, I know I am better off.

The first time I heard about the concept of perception was in one of my Political Science classes. I listened intently as the professor spoke about how perception could lead to war. This was because one person may perceive something differently from another person. I found the whole idea of perception to be quite intriguing and absolutely fascinating.

To demonstrate the concept of perception, I have come up with a simple exercise. Take a look at the symbol below. What do you see?

What is the name of this symbol?

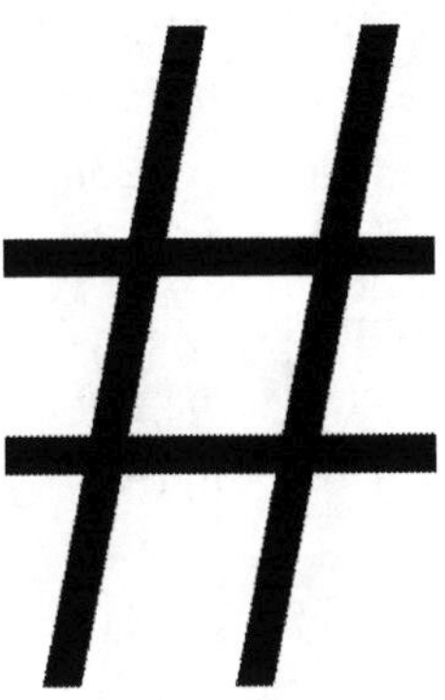

The symbol on the last page can mean different things to different people. The symbol can be perceived as a hashtag symbol, the number sign, the US pound sign, or a tic-tac-toe board. This simple exercise demonstrates how one thing can be seen differently by different people. Therefore, it is my hope that by the end of this chapter, you will be able to fully grasp the concept of perception and be able to incorporate it into your everyday life.

Another exercise in perception is one that most people have encountered. It revolves around the dilemma of a glass containing water that reaches about 50% of its holding capacity. Some will say the glass is half-full; while others will say that the glass is half-empty. Look at the picture below.

Do you see a glass half-full? Or do you see the glass half-empty?

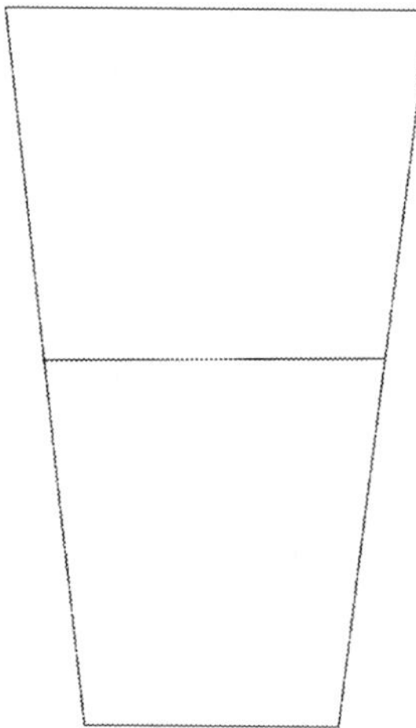

Depending on whether you see the glass as being half-full or half-empty will then lead others to make assumptions about you, the observer of the glass. Some may assume that you are an optimist if you view the glass as being half-full. Some may assume that you are a pessimist if you see the glass as being half-empty. Even though that may not be the case at all.

Paradigm Shift

The quote at the beginning of this chapter is a good way of looking at the concept of perception. According to Wayne Dyer, "When you change the way you look at things, the things you look at change." You don't need fancy glasses, a pair of binoculars, or a telescope to change your perception. For the change in perception that occurs is done with the mind. It can be viewed as a paradigm shift. This is when one begins to realize that there are different ways of looking at any given thing, situation, concept, problem, etc.

When I was trying to begin a new life after my divorce, I met up with Nova—a friend I had acquired while in university—for lunch. She was telling me how great everyone we had known in school was doing. Nova then informed me that Scarlet—our mutual friend—was now a corporate attorney who worked for one of the biggest automobile manufacturers in the country. Scarlett was also happily married with two amazing kids. She also lived in a beautiful mansion in the best county in the state. I was extremely happy for Scarlet. However, I also felt like an utter failure. Primarily due to the fact that I was crashing on my friend's sofa and didn't have a job. To top it all off, my British Law degree and Canadian Political Science degrees were just two pieces of paper I had stuffed in an envelope somewhere in my suitcase.

Just when I thought I couldn't feel any worse, Nova's phone rang. It was Scarlet. I guess she had heard us talking about her good fortune through the cosmic airwaves. Nova handed me the phone and said, "Scarlet wants to say hi." I felt myself drowning in despair as Scarlet cheerfully chirped the question I most dreaded, "How are you?" I then proceeded to tell her the same story I had told countless others; that I had recently gotten divorced, was jobless, and living on my friend's sofa. Scarlet then assured me that things would eventually work out. She also told me that things are not always what they appear to be. Then Scarlet said something that I will never forget. She said, "I bet you're still skinny." I was taken aback by her comment. Her words shook me out of my coma of depression. Here I was droning on and on about what I didn't have in comparison to her, and all she wanted was to be skinny again.

A few years later, Nova told me that Scarlett had gotten a divorce. Scarlet had also relocated to a new country with her kids. My mind flashed back to the conversation I had on the phone with Scarlet a few years prior when she had said, "Things are not always as they appear to be." This may have been Scarlet's way of alluding to the fact that her marriage was not as solid as it appeared to be and may have in fact been on shaky ground. She may well have been on the verge of a divorce herself. From her perspective, I may have been living the life of a free woman; which may have been what she wanted. In her mind, I might have been better off than her, and to top it all off, I was still skinny. That was a realization of seismic proportions for me—a paradigm shift.

Another incident comes to mind when I think about how impactful a paradigm shift can be to a person's outlook on life. One day, I was talking to a kind and handsome gentleman named James. I was telling him about my mosquito allergy that I was plagued with. He listened intently as I told him that when I got bitten, I would swell up, the bite would darken, and eventually leave a mark on my skin. The mark would blend into my skin but you would still be able to see a small scar upon close inspection. James simply smiled and said, "Scars just give your skin character." What? I couldn't believe it! He saw my scars as adding character to my skin. Instantly, a paradigm shift occurred in my mind/reality/future. James was able to perceive my negative attribute as something positive. I thought to myself, "Where have you been all my life?" Needless to say, I married him.

Sometimes the smallest thing can result in a change of epic proportions. This maybe because once you are able to see things in a different light, it is difficult to unsee it. When your perception of situations, concepts, and problems change, your views on the issues may also change. Inadvertently, once your views on issues change, the world as you know it may also undergo changes due to the change in your perception that was created by the paradigm shift that you had experienced.

The Pygmalion Effect

Have you ever heard of the Pygmalion effect? It's a concept that is studied and taught in leadership. It's when the behaviors and performance of followers are determined by their leaders' attitudes, treatment, and expectations of them (Lussier & Achua, 2014, p.47). Basically, if the leader expects the followers to succeed, they will; and if the leader expects the followers to fail, they will. The Pygmalion effect is also known as a self-fulfilling prophecy. This is because the perception of the situation contributes to the success or failure of the situation.

Pet owners are famous for demonstrating the Pygmalion effect with their fur babies. Brian and Britany—a couple I know—have a small-breed dog named Jackson. Jackson is known for relieving himself in my house—otherwise known as "accidents"— whenever they come over for a visit. In fact, I am always on the lookout for his "accidents." However, Brian and Britany seem to be totally oblivious to the fact that Jackson does this every time he came for a visit. One day, Brian and Britany were telling me how Jackson gets blamed for "accidents" when they go to visit their friend Claudia. They claimed that it was more than likely that Claudia's dog Bailey was the one responsible for the "accidents." I just looked at them in utter disbelief and smiled. I couldn't understand how they were not able to see that it may very well have been Jackson who had the "accidents" and not Bailey. Afterall, it was in the realm of possibilities since Jackson was always relieving himself in my house.

A few questions come to mind when trying to unravel the Jackson "accident" quandary. The first question is, does Jackson use my house as a toilet bowl because I expect him to? The second question is, does he do it because no matter what he does, he will always be perceived as being a "good boy" by his parents? In the end, I have to ponder whether my attitudes and expectations are responsible for fueling Jackson's behavior. Thus, the Pygmalion effect seems like the paradox of the "chicken and the egg" dilemma when it comes to dissecting the implications in relation to Jackson. Thus, I can only speculate at this point since Jackson is a dog and can't communicate his actions or intentions to me. However, I can change my attitude and expectations for him the next time he comes over. Maybe that would lead to a different outcome. Hence, the Pygmalion effect.

The fact that the Pygmalion effect can have an influence on the way in which one sees a particular situation is quite intriguing. Being aware that there is a possibility that one's attitudes and expectations of an issue may actually contribute to its outcome is very useful information. It may give an individual insight in to the outcome of a particular situation, problem, or issue. The concept may also shed light on how one's own expectations may influence and shape their perception on a particular issue. Once one becomes aware of their role in shaping the outcome of a given situation, one can then learn to utilize it to their benefit. Subsequently, being able to master and harness the power of the Pygmalion effect may ultimately lead to paradigm shifts and changes in perception.

Reframing Perception

Reframing is a concept that is used in mediation. This is where the mediator would rephrase the words that one party used to make it sound more appealing to the other person. It's a very useful skill to have—especially when dealing with individuals who are not capable of being in the same room with each other. Sometimes, the parties may use profanity or negative terms because they are very frustrated about a situation. However, a skilled mediator has the ability—as a neutral third party—to repackage the words and make them more pleasant. So, for example, one party may exclaim, "There's no way that egomaniacal jerk is taking my book collection! He can have the worthless pen collection." A skilled mediator would then reframe this message by saying, "Well, she's willing to give you the priceless pen collection. However, she would like to keep the book collection." Simply stated, when one reframes something, it is repackaged in a way that becomes palatable for the other person to absorb.

Unquestionably, the concept of reframing, coupled with the knowledge of perception, will allow one to better understand situations. This is because if an individual can comprehend that there is more than one way of looking at a situation and is able to reframe it in a positive way—they will then be on their way to being able to tackle difficult issues. Furthermore, by combining perception and reframing, one will gain a very useful skill when faced with conflict.

There have been numerous times in my life when I reframed perceptions. At the time, though, I wasn't aware that I was reframing. However, they say that hindsight is 20/20. Now that I am older and looking back on my experiences, I can clearly see where these concepts were used in a variety of situations.

My earliest memory of reframing was when I was in the third grade. I was at recess, standing at the tetherball court. This was a game that was on most Canadian elementary school playgrounds. I was eight years old at the time. A girl named Hilda approached me. She then asked, "Do you want to come and bully kids with me?" I looked at her and responded, "No", and I then walked away. I remember thinking to myself, "Why would anyone want to bully kids?" In my mind, I would not want to be bullied, so why would I want to bully someone else? I also thought about the little kids wanting to have fun at recess. No one wanted to be bothered at recess or any other time for that matter. As well, I didn't want to spend my time bullying other children on the playground, I wanted to play. All in all, I recall thinking that Hilda's suggestion was pretty silly.

Inadvertently, I had reframed the idea of playground bullying by looking at it from the perception of the kids who would have been the target of the bullying. I had placed myself in the position of the potential victim. I had also pondered bullying from my perspective and the implications it would have on me. In a nutshell, I was able to perceive the playground bully recruitment encounter from a few different perspectives. Ultimately, by utilizing the concept of reframing, I was able to decide against becoming a playground bully.

Another story that comes to mind about perception and reframing takes me back to the time when I worked as a cashier at a grocery store. I was a cashier while in university. Even though I was a cashier, I had to help put away returns, and whatever else needed to be done. One evening after closing, I had to help with the returns. I was rounding the corner to the produce section when I heard Sam— the produce manager— proclaim, "Look, I'm Joy!" As I turned the corner, I saw him holding two melons up to his chest. His audience of three male employees starred at me with a look of embarrassment painted on their faces. Humiliation was the only thing I remember feeling as I stood there; as if my feet were glued to the floor. Sam turned around and laughed when he saw me.

After I left the store that evening and was able to regain control of my thoughts; Sam and the embarrassing fruit incident filled my mind. I realized that he was older, single, and had worked at that store for many years. My analysis of him concluded that he didn't have much of a life outside of the store. In fact, the store was his life. Arguably, even though Sam had acted inappropriately, he may have been looking for friendships from his younger male employees. When I pondered reporting him to the store manager, I realized that Sam would probably justify his behavior by claiming it was a joke. He may have said that his gestures with the melons weren't meant in a sexual way. Sam may have even believed that I had taken his actions out of context and had perceived his playfulness in the wrong way. Justifiably, I knew how his actions made me feel—my feelings were my own—and I didn't feel good about his infantile behavior.

After lengthy internal dialogue and mental anguish, I came to a few realizations. First of all, I realized that I was new at the store. I had only worked there for a few weeks; whereas Sam had worked there for a number of years. Secondly, I realized that I was a teenager; whereas Sam was a middle-aged man. Thirdly, it would be easier for me to find another job; whereas Sam would probably have a hard time finding another job. My internal analysis helped me to clarify my perceptions about the situation.

In the final analysis, I quit the grocery store a week later. I was able to reframe Sam's inappropriate behavior as that of a middle-aged man trying to gain approval from his employees, as opposed to him being an old pervert. Interestingly, by perceiving Sam as a lonely man, I was able to walk away from that job and move on with my life. Don't misunderstand me, Sam was 100% wrong for his deviant behavior. He had no reason to act in such a terrible manner. However, I didn't want to cause Sam more harm than I had to. I had no intention of making my grocery store job a long-term career. Afterall, I was a full-time student, in a new city, pursuing a university education. For me; I had a bright radiant future ahead of me. On the other hand, I knew that Sam perceived his job as his career and safety net. In contrast, Sam thought of his job as a long-term endeavor. One that he would be able to retire and collect a pension from. Therefore, by walking away from the grocery store, I actually did Sam a favor. At least that's the way I choose to frame my decision.

When you reframe perception, it can change the way others see things as well. One such situation occurred years ago when I was visiting some relatives in Toronto, Canada. At the time, I was living in Charleston, SC. Leo—a family friend—was also visiting. There were a few of us gathered at the table when Leo asked, "Isn't it racist in the southern States?" I looked at him and answered, "The most racism I've ever experienced has been in Canada." Leo was shocked at my response. I proceeded to tell him the following story.

One day, I was in the downtown area of Toronto and I needed directions. I was trying to find a street and was not sure which way to go. To my relief, there was an older Caucasian woman sitting at a bus stop. She looked like a sweet little old lady. Like someone's grandmother from a cookie commercial. Convinced that she would help me, I walked over to her. I smiled and chimed, "Excuse me. Can you please help me?" She stared straight ahead.

To my bewilderment, she didn't answer. Due to her age, I deliberated that she may have been hard of hearing. So, I stepped a little closer and using a louder tone I queried, "Excuse me. Can you please help me?" She then turned her head, looked at me, and postulated, "I don't help ******* (insert N word here)!" Shocked and confused, I was speechless. It was the first time that I had ever been called the N word. No one had ever mistaken me for anything other than a "Paki" before. After starring at her for a few seconds, I quickly walked away from her. Eventually, I encountered another stranger who kindly helped me navigate the streets of Toronto.

Leo just sat there with a stunned look on his face. He didn't realize that Toronto had people who were so openly racist. So, by reframing his image of the city he lived in, he was able to perceive it differently. I wanted him to understand that based on my personal experience the Southern states were no more racist than the very multi-cultural city in which he resided. At the end of the day, I wanted to drive home the point that it is not the geography of the city that makes it racist— it is the people who live in the city that make it racist.

As you can clearly see, perception is a very powerful concept. Once you learn how to utilize it to your benefit, you will be able to influence the way other people see things. Indeed, everyone perceives things in their own way. However, learning how to consciously help individuals see things from a certain perspective may enable you to persuade them to view things from a different angle. By doing this, you may enable them to set their vision ablaze and unite in agreement on matters such as race, gender, and violence.

Exercise 1

What is your ***favorite drink***? Picture it in the glass below. Do you see the glass half-full? Or do you see the glass half-empty?

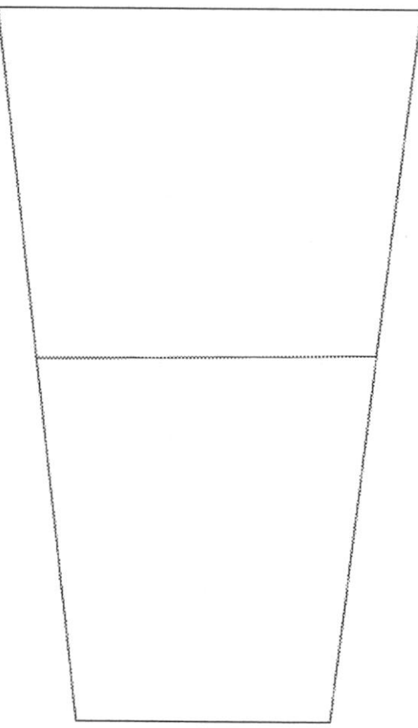

Exercise 2

What is your ***least favorite drink***? Picture it in the glass below. Do you see the glass half-full? Or do you see the glass half-empty?

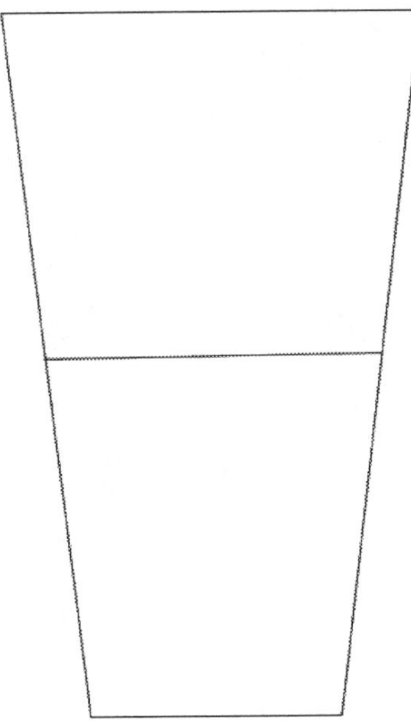

Exercise 3

What do you think the image below is? Fill in the blank with what you perceive the image to be. Color the picture to clarify your perception of it. If you don't have anything to color with, you can simply visualize it in your mind's eye.

I see a ____.

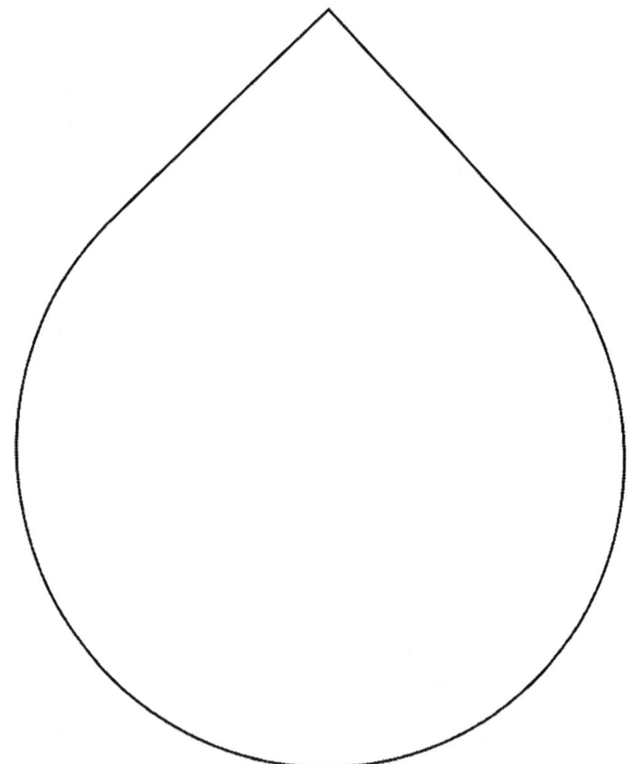

Answer

Chapter 3 Word Search

T	A	R	G	E	N	T	I	R	A	O	B	C	S	S	G	F	K	L	H
H	P	S	R	A	T	T	E	Y	E	S	G	C	A	J	O	O	N	P	O
O	S	N	O	I	T	A	T	C	E	P	X	E	S	I	T	C	A	S	M
U	A	I	T	T	T	F	K	D	X	O	P	L	O	G	U	R	W	F	A
G	T	F	E	I	B	W	I	B	I	L	T	M	A	T	A	S	O	N	N
P	E	R	C	E	P	T	I	O	N	S	W	D	Q	D	T	S	T	I	R
T	R	T	B	A	M	U	H	V	Q	E	P	I	I	V	T	E	A	W	E
S	S	T	A	T	E	M	E	N	T	F	I	G	P	A	I	I	I	A	L
F	G	P	A	N	C	E	S	T	R	Y	M	T	A	M	T	M	R	P	A
N	N	I	F	L	E	D	T	U	I	S	E	O	C	I	U	I	R	Z	X
E	I	E	R	C	I	S	E	F	H	S	A	G	T	N	D	S	O	W	A
R	M	I	H	I	D	F	T	I	V	E	X	U	O	D	E	T	L	L	T
E	A	S	J	U	V	G	F	E	T	Y	B	E	O	J	S	E	N	O	I
N	R	S	K	Y	B	T	C	O	N	V	E	R	S	A	T	I	O	N	O
Y	F	E	L	T	H	N	U	T	F	U	B	G	I	C	J	B	V	K	N
E	E	N	Y	R	Y	J	I	L	V	J	B	H	M	U	R	R	O	R	Y
S	R	G	R	E	T	C	E	F	F	E	N	O	I	L	A	M	G	Y	P
C	Y	D	E	E	P	B	R	E	A	T	H	I	N	G	H	K	S	H	U

Words To Find		
PERCEPTION	REFRAMING	PARADIGM SHIFT
ATTITUDES	EXPECTATIONS	PYGMALION EFFECT

Chapter 3 Pangram

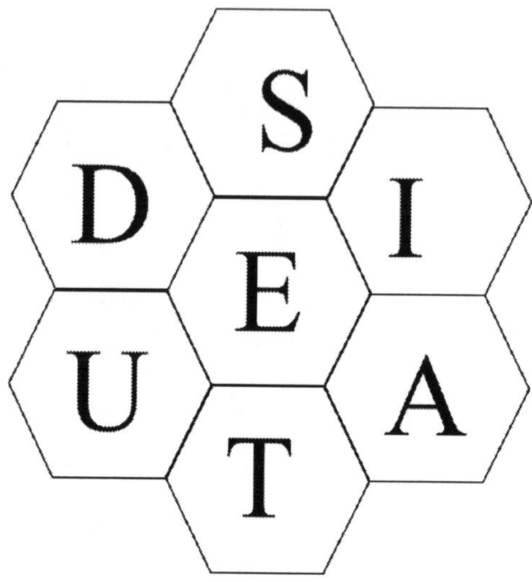

Use all the letters in the pangram to create a word from chapter 3. You can use letters multiple times. Write the word you made below.

Chapter 3 Word Scramble

Unscramble the following words.

Scrambled Word	Unscrambled Word
petpincero	
adigmapr hisft	
gamlionpy feetfc	
gamerinfr	
cnatiostexep	
tasteduti	

Answers

Exercise 3 Possible Answers: Teardrop, water droplet, or flame.

Chapter 3 Word Search Answers

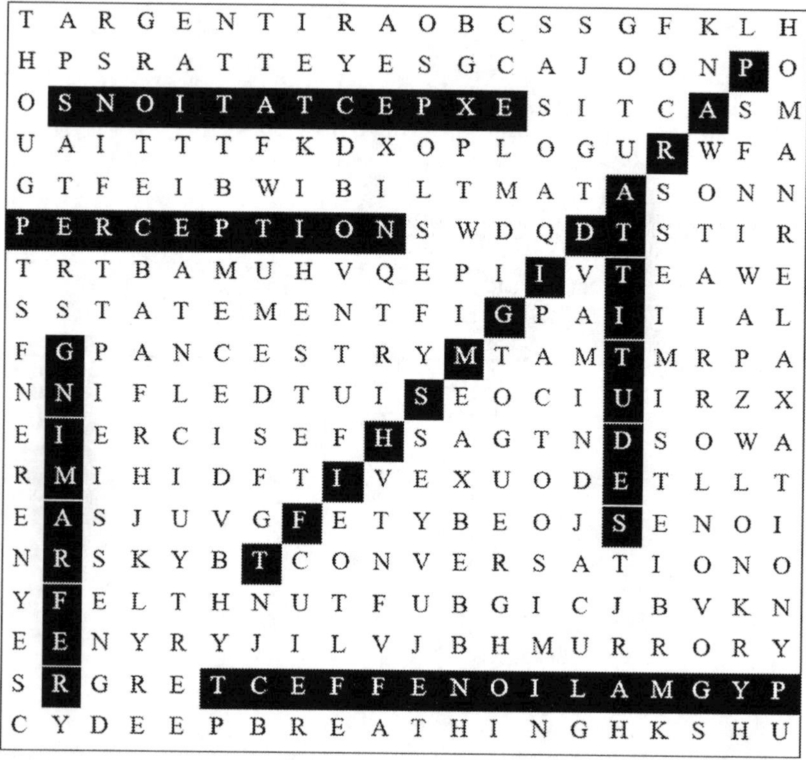

Chapter 3 Pangram Answer

Attitudes

Chapter 3 Word Scramble Answers

Unscrambled Word
perception
paradigm shift
pygmalion effect
reframing
expectations
attitudes

CHAPTER 4

Inflame Insight

"Our lives are a sum total of the choices we have made."
-Wayne Dyer

The Big Picture

A teenage girl named Ella had gotten pregnant at 16. When her family found out, she became their disgrace. Her father tied her to a tree and beat her with a belt. Ella was made to feel ashamed. Her parents also forced her to marry the boy responsible, Troy. Ella's marriage was riddled with violence. Her new husband had a temper, abused alcohol, and hated the responsibility of being married with a child. After a few years of abuse, her family decided that she would be better off without Troy. So, they then forced her to get divorced. This left Ella twice disgraced. She was now the black sheep divorcee of the family.

Ella hated herself and her daughter Eve. The child only reminded her of her disgrace. Every time Ella looked at Eve, she wished she were dead. Ella transferred all of her anger and hate on to Eve. As a result, Eve was verbally and physically abused by Ella. Ella was unable to give any love to Eve as she had none to give. Needless to say, Eve and Ella were unable to have a good relationship. When Eve was old enough to be on her own, she left home. In the end, Ella saw her unwanted pregnancy as a life sentence of shame and viewed Eve as her punishment.

Another teenage girl named Ava also got pregnant at 16. When her parents found out, they were a bit surprised. However, they were very supportive of her, and they wanted to make sure that Ava was able to finish high school. So, while Ava was pregnant, she took her high school classes online. After her baby, Sarah, was born, she continued to take her classes online. With her parents help and encouragement, she graduated high school.

Ava and her boyfriend Matt—the father of her child—decided to get married shortly after she had graduated. They both loved and cared for Sarah. Ava was able to love her daughter, Sarah, because she had received love from her parents and therefore had love to give.

Furthermore, Ava went on to graduate from college. This was due to the help she received from both her parents and Matt's parents. Sarah grew up knowing she was loved by her parents and grandparents. Sarah's grandparents would help to care for her whenever Ava or Matt had to work or had classes. This symbiotic relationship benefitted everyone; as the parents, grandparents, and child were all able to bond and work as a family unit. Subsequently, Sarah was able to secure a good job after graduating. She was able to be a good mother because of her support system. In the end, Sarah saw her pregnancy as a stepping stone and not as a stumbling block; which gave her the drive to embrace motherhood.

Mila—a woman in her forties—had done everything right according to her judgmental family. She had received her MBA (Masters of Business Administration) in her twenties. After graduate school she had landed a good job as an accountant. Mila then shopped, travelled, and acquired worldly possessions.

In her thirties she got married. Her new husband—Jake—had gotten a job offer in a foreign country. They decided that it would be a good opportunity for both of them, so they packed their bags and moved away from their friends and family. They relished in their new environment. They travelled to neighboring countries, tried new foods, and learned new languages. Everything was so exciting and new.

A few years went by and the newness and excitement of Mila and Jake's move wore off. They were now ready to have children. However, they were not able to conceive a child on their own so they started fertility treatments. After numerous tries they were still unable to conceive a child. Mila grew depressed and withdrew from her friends. Jake blamed her for their inability to have a child. Jake's family couldn't understand why Mila couldn't get pregnant.

Mila started to feel worthless. She thought about all the women who had children but didn't want them. She thought about all the teenagers who had unwanted pregnancies. She thought about all the people who had more children than they knew what to do with. Why couldn't she have one—just one. What was wrong with her? Why was she broken?

Life in a foreign country became unbearable. Mila and Jake fought constantly. Mila wanted to move back to her country of origin. She didn't want to live in a foreign land anymore. She needed to have a support system. Jake finally agreed that they needed to move back home.

A few months later, they arrived back to the country they loved. Unfortunately, the damage was already done to their relationship. The infertility issue was just too huge of a burden. It hung over their heads like a dark cloud. Everywhere they went, it followed. The issue was also compounded by the persistent inquiry into their personal lives by their friends and family. Unfortunately, Mila and Jake divorced shortly after they arrived back to their native land.

One year after the divorce, Mila ran in to Jake at the grocery store. To her amazement he was holding a baby. Jake smiled at her and said, "How are you?" Mila smiled and replied, "I'm good. Thank you." They spoke pleasantly to each other. However, it was what was left unspoken that would later haunt Mila.

Jake had not remarried; however, he had fathered a child. In contrast, Mila would have been stigmatized by her family if she had done that. Why was it okay for him to have a child out of wedlock? Furthermore, why did she have to finish college, have a career, and get married before she could have a child? She had done all of that—yet there she was, childless. Why did society expect so much from her as a woman? She left the store that day wondering how different her life would have been if she had gotten pregnant as a teenager.

Women are blamed for unwanted pregnancies or lack of pregnancies; even though the fault may not lay with them. Women are judged for having children too young or for not having children at all. However, if a woman is able to get an education, land a stable career, and wrangle a husband, then she is considered a success. The reality of the situation is that life doesn't always happen in that order. Things come up; plans change. Some women may have a child first, then get married, and then go to college later in their lives. Some women may get married first, finish college next, then have children. Some women may choose to adopt and not get married. All in all, children are a blessing regardless of how they come into the world.

The Pregnancy Trio is what I call the above stories. The three women—Ella, Ava, and Mila—were from three different races. One woman was of

Caucasian descent, one woman was of African descent, and one woman was of Asian descent. Can you figure out what race they each belong to? Why do you think what you do? Regardless of what race they belonged to, they are all part of the human race. As human beings, women need to be treated with kindness and consideration regardless of the status of their reproductive system.

Gender is the primary issue at play when it comes to pregnancy and infertility. In recent years, infertility has become a major issue for countless women regardless of their race. So, we as a society need to approach the issue of gender and infertility with understanding and may need to revisit our judgmental attitudes when faced with the issue of pregnancy.

In mediation, looking at the big picture is a method that is used to shed insight into a situation. Sometimes one needs to zoom out of a situation in order to see what is important. When one has zoomed out of a pregnancy scenario, they would be able to see that there are human beings at the core of the issue. Therefore, the situation should be approached with care and compassion. In the long run, dealing with the situation of a pregnancy will have an impact on multiple lives. Thus, it needs to be handled with care.

The quote at the beginning of the of the chapter is quite relevant when looking at the big picture of life. As Wayne Dyer claimed, "Our lives are a sum total of the choices we have made." Therefore, if we want to change our lives, we may need to make different choices. As we make different choices, we will see that the big picture of our lives will start to change as well.

This can be demonstrated with health. If one is overweight, one can simply start making different choices. So, by simply choosing to eat healthy foods instead of unhealthy foods, one can lose weight. Hence, one can go from being overweight to achieving a healthy weight. One would have then changed from being unhealthy to healthy; thus, changing one's overall quality of life. Ultimately, small choices can impact the big picture of one's health.

By making small choices throughout one's day/week/month, one can dramatically impact one's life. Fundamentally, small choices can lead to big changes. Thus, it is my hope that by the end of this chapter, you will be able to see how your choices can impact your ability to deal with difficult and complex issues such as race, gender, and violence.

Separate the Individual from the Issue

In the book *Getting to Yes,* the authors discuss separating the people from the problem during negotiations. According to Fisher and Ury (2011) "The basic approach is to deal with the people as human beings and with the problem on its merits" (p.41). I agree with their method, however, I don't label everything as a problem when it comes to having difficult conversations. That is why I prefer to say that one should separate the individual from the issue. So, when having difficult conversations about race, gender, and violence one needs to deal with the individuals as human beings whilst tackling the issues based on the relevant facts; free from personal feelings and judgements.

Without a doubt, this is no easy task. In fact, being able to separate the individual from the issue is sometimes very difficult to do. However, with some practice, one can rise to the challenge. Once you have tackled the task a few times, you will find that you would have become quite proficient at separating the individual from the issue.

One evening while dozing off on my sofa, the phone rang. I answered it, and the voice on the other end said, "Hi, my name is Vicky and I'm having an affair with your husband Vlad." Not quite sure if I was still sleeping, I responded, "What?" Unfortunately, to my dismay, I had awakened from my dream to what would become a living nightmare.

A few weeks prior, I had flown back to Canada to have surgery. I had rented a small place to stay during my recovery. Needless to say, weeks later I was still in some pain as I slowly recovered from the procedure. So, I was pretty groggy when I answered the phone that night, as I was still pumped up on pain medication. During the infamous "phone call", Vicky would go on to tell me that she had been with Vlad for two years. I was stunned to say the least.

After I finished talking to Vicky, I immediately called Vlad to find out what the heck was going on! He answered in a subdued tone and admitted to everything. In that moment, it was as if someone has turned on the light in a dark room. I was finally able to see clearly. All of the puzzle pieces were starting to fit together in my mind. Vlad and I had been having problems for a while. So, all the fights, lies, and erratic behavior now made sense. He had been living a secret double life.

I spent the remainder of that week getting my stuff together to go back to the Bahamas. During that week, I was also able to get a handle on the situation by figuring out how to separate the individuals from the issue. The issue was my marriage and the individuals were Vlad and Vicky. Vlad was the one who had made the commitment to me. Vicky didn't know me. Vlad was the one that was at fault for breaking his vows, not Vicky. Don't misunderstand me, Vicky shouldn't have gotten involved with a married man. However, Vlad was the one who betrayed me.

The next week I flew back to the Bahamas and stayed at a hotel. I also went to visit Vicky. She had given me her address and wanted me to come and speak with her. So, I did.

When I arrived at Vicky's house, I was surprised to find her mother, brother, and friend there as well. As I sat there in the red and white fabric chair—I felt as if I was having an out-of-body experience. It was surreal; something out of a dream/nightmare. I listened to all of them as they told me about how Vlad would have Sunday dinner with them. How Vlad would hang out with Vicky's dad and smoke cigars. How Vlad and Vicky's brother were friends. The stories seemed to flow on and on....

My blinders were taken off. I was finally able to see the person I was really married to for the first time. Vicky and her band of supporters had given me the gift of clarity to see that Vlad was a liar and deceiver. I couldn't reconcile how one person could be so horrible. How could he have lived this double life? The marriage would never be able to recover from the deceit and ended shortly after.

Many people wondered why I wasn't mad at Vicky. Afterall, she was the "other woman." It was difficult for people to understand why I didn't hold her accountable. I would tell them that Vicky was not the one who was married to me. Vlad was the one who had walked out of the marriage. In the end, I was able to separate the issue from the individuals. As a result of this, I was able to glean insight in to the matter and gained the strength to walk away.

As the saying goes, "What goes around, comes around." Years later, I had heard that Vlad and Vicky had reunited. The two had even gotten engaged. However, Vlad called the engagement off because he couldn't see himself marrying Vicky. Vlad had told Merrick—a friend of his—that he couldn't trust her. Vlad had stated, "How can I trust her? She had an affair with a married man." Wow! How righteous of him to see the error of her ways. In truth, I think Vicky was the one who dodged the bullet in that situation. In actuality, Vlad walking away from Vicky was probably the best thing that could have happened to her. (Refer to chapter 3 if you need a refresher on Vlad's troubles.) All in all, everything worked out in the end.

Outcomes

Most people have probably heard of a win/win outcome. As outlined by Covey (2013) "Win/win is based on the paradigm that there is plenty for everyone, that one person's success is not achieved at the expense or exclusion of the success of others" (p.218). I fully agree with this statement. For me, the best outcome of a discussion is a win/win outcome because it satisfies everyone involved and no one feels like they have lost at the expense of the other person's success. If everyone is happy with the outcome, then the issue would have been handled in the best way possible.

There are alternative outcomes to a win/win. There are also win/lose, lose/win, and lose/lose. These other outcomes are not as desirable as a win/win because they leave one party unhappy or dissatisfied. Once you start to understand the four outcomes, you will begin to see them appear throughout your life and circumstances.

Win/Lose Scenario

Harper and Layla were sisters. Harper was older than Layla, as she was the product of their mother's first marriage. Layla was the product of their mother's second marriage. Their mother always favored Layla because she was still married to Layla's father. Whenever Layla would get in trouble, she would blame it on Harper. Their mother would join Layla in using Harper as a scapegoat for almost everything that happened in Layla's life. Harper had reached her limit and eventually moved out of state when she was old enough.

One day, Harper's mother called her on the phone to tell her that Layla had snuck her boyfriend into the house the night before. Her mother was shaken by the incident because she initially mistook him for an intruder. Her mother seemed very upset.

Harper told her mother that she would fly home. This however was no cheap matter. Harper had to pay an exorbitant price for the last-minute flight. Luckily, she had just gotten a credit card in the mail. Without giving it a second thought, Harper immediately booked her ticket even though it maxed out her credit card. She thought her sister and mother needed her, so she was willing to pay the price.

The next day Harper was back home. Before she could put her bag down Layla spouted, "Now you do something so that mom won't be mad at me anymore." Harper was taken aback by Layla's anger towards her. Layla then thundered, "Do you know what mom said last night? She said that her other daughter would never have done this!" Harper was suddenly hit with the realization that she had been stuck in a zero-sum game of win/lose with Layla her entire life. Layla was always winning as long as Harper was losing.

By the next day, Layla and their mother had reunited in their cause to make Harper the loser in their game of life. Harper watched in utter disbelief as Layla and their mother went shopping. Harper observed them drive off and wondered why she had even bothered to come back home. She felt like a gambler that had gone to Las Vegas; in the beginning so full of hope and credit, however, by the end broke and full of regret. Just like in Las Vegas the house always won at the expense of the gambler.

Lose/Win Scenario

Owen's parents had gotten divorced primarily because his father had an affair and had moved out. In fact, his father had even gotten remarried. The woman he had married had a child named Zoey, who was the same age as Owen. He knew Zoey because she was in the same grade as him and went to the same school as he did. Zoey now also had the same last name as him—Smith—because his father had adopted her.

Owen was only eight years old at the time. The new school year had recently begun and Zoey was in his class. Whenever the teacher took attendance, he would hear their names called. The teacher would say, "Owen Smith" followed by "Zoey Smith." Various teachers would ask if they were related or if they were siblings. Owen would only shrug his shoulders in response as he did not know how to explain their situation.

Owen couldn't comprehend why his father had abandoned him and his mother to go and live with Zoey and her mother. Was Zoey better than him? Was Zoey now his father's favorite child? Was Zoey more deserving of attention? In Owen's mind, Zoey had won his father's love. Owen was caught in a lose/win spider web of emotion. He began to believe that he had lost and Zoey had won. Sadly, Owen never recovered. Even as an adult, Owen continued to think that Zoey was better than him and more deserving of love than he was.

Lose/Lose Scenario

Chloe had been dating Clayton for a few years. He had gotten to know her family and friends. He had even gone on vacation with Chloe's family before. Chloe's social network loved him. They even had a name for the couple they called them "Clay-Lo." Everyone was expecting them to get married. They were so perfect for each other.

However, one day it all changed. Chloe's friend called her to inform her that Clayton was dating someone else as well. Apparently, some people had seen him having dinner with his other girlfriend. Chloe called Clayton to confront him. He verified that he did have another girlfriend. He also proceeded to break up with her on the phone.

Chloe instantly became consumed with rage. How dare he embarrass her like that. Nobody makes a fool of her! If she was going to lose something she loved—their relationship—then he was going to lose something he loved—his sports car. Clayton's prized possession was his red sports car. He took exceptional care of his car as he washed it, waxed it, and cleaned it weekly.

Chloe grabbed a baseball bat from the garage and drove over to Clayton's house. There, parked on the driveway, was Clayton's red car. She parked and approached the vehicle. She then proceeded to smash the tail lights with the bat. Swing after swing, she dented and smashed Clayton's car. Chloe was enraptured in the dance of the lose/lose.

Chloe had lost herself in vengeance. For her, destroying Clayton's car was the only way to get back at him for cheating on her and then dumping her. He had loved his car just as much as she had loved him. She justified her behavior by claiming that she had smashed his car the same way he had smashed her heart. In the end, Chloe made sure that they were both losers in the game of love.

Win/Win Scenario

Elsa was a typical 12-year-old. She loved being on devices. If her phone battery ever died; it would be cause for distress. A few weeks ago, her cousin

Enya had told her that her father—Paul—had broken her computer with a hammer. Paul had gotten so frustrated at Enya because she had gotten caught up watching videos on the internet. In a nutshell, Enya was distraught about losing her computer.

One night, Elsa's mom—Camila—had found out that she was texting on her phone when she was supposed to be asleep. This was because Camilla found the phone lying beside Elsa in the morning. Camilla was at her wits end.

Before breakfast, Camila went out to the garage and retrieved a hammer. She then put the hammer on the kitchen table beside Elsa's phone. Camilla then called Elsa into the kitchen. Elsa had a look of horror wash over her face when she saw the hammer next to her phone. Camilla looked at Elsa and snarled, "Do you remember what Uncle Paul did to Enya's computer?" Elsa murmured, "Yes."

Camilla sat Elsa down and explained to her that she needed to sleep at night so that she could focus on school, friends, and family during the day. She also reiterated to Elsa that she loved her and only wanted the best for her. Camila also told Elsa that if she didn't follow the rules, she would lose her phone privileges. Camilla outlined that Elsa would have to leave her phone in Camilla's room at night to charge. The reason for this, Camilla explained to Elsa, was to eliminate the temptation of using the phone at night. Elsa agreed to the terms her mother had laid out for her to abide by. Camilla and Elsa had now begun a game of tech tennis in which both players scored love/love. Elsa apologized for her behavior. She also expressed her gratitude to her mother for not "freaking out" and breaking her phone with a hammer.

In summary, Camilla and Elsa had reached a win/win outcome. Elsa was able to keep her phone privileges and Camilla was able to keep her cool. By using dialogue instead of violence, they were able to move forward with clarity and understanding.

Everyone can start to make choices that will lead to positive changes in their lives. Simply by focusing on the big picture one can zoom out of any situation to see what's really important in the end. When one can separate the individual from the issue, it will allow them to truly focus on the matters and not the judgements surrounding the issue. The ultimate outcome that one should strive for in any situation is a win/win outcome.

When everyone feels satisfied with the outcome, the issue would have been handled in the best way possible. Therefore, by understanding these techniques, one would be able to equip themself with some much-needed knowledge that would enable them to embark on difficult conversations about race, gender, and violence.

Exercise 1

Write about a time you had a conflict. Now, separate the individual from the issue.

Exercise 2

Write about a time you had a win/win outcome.

Exercise 3

Visualize ***what you would look like*** when you have achieved a win/win outcome. You can draw a picture in the box if you want or you can simply visualize it in your mind's eye.

Chapter 4 Word Search

T	C	R	G	E	C	O	N	F	L	I	C	T	S	S	G	F	K	L	H
H	A	S	R	A	T	T	E	Y	E	S	G	C	A	L	O	T	N	W	O
O	L	L	A	E	E	T	S	I	P	A	G	Y	S	I	T	L	E	S	C
U	M	I	T	T	T	F	K	D	X	O	P	L	O	S	U	A	W	F	O
T	T	F	E	I	B	W	I	B	I	L	T	M	A	T	I	U	O	N	N
C	W	Q	U	E	S	I	I	O	N	S	W	D	Q	E	E	D	T	I	V
O	R	T	B	A	M	U	G	V	E	E	P	I	O	N	T	I	A	W	E
M	S	T	A	T	E	M	E	P	T	F	I	A	P	A	P	V	I	A	R
E	Z	P	A	N	C	R	A	S	I	L	V	E	A	M	E	I	R	P	S
S	X	I	F	L	E	R	T	U	I	C	E	O	C	O	O	D	R	Z	A
I	X	I	R	C	A	O	E	H	C	S	T	G	T	N	P	N	O	W	T
R	V	I	H	T	A	S	K	P	H	E	X	U	O	D	T	I	L	L	I
R	B	S	E	U	V	G	Y	E	T	Y	B	E	R	J	Y	E	N	O	O
O	N	S	R	Y	R	E	S	P	O	I	S	S	U	E	T	I	O	N	N
R	M	E	L	T	H	N	U	T	F	U	B	G	I	C	J	B	V	K	M
E	W	N	Y	R	Y	J	I	L	V	J	B	H	M	U	R	R	O	R	Y
S	E	G	R	E	U	M	K	E	B	N	I	W	N	I	W	G	U	E	T
C	Y	D	I	A	L	O	G	U	E	Y	H	I	O	G	H	K	S	H	U

Words To Find		
SEPARATE	INDIVIDUAL	ISSUE
WIN WIN	BIG PICTURE	OUTCOMES

Chapter 4 Pangram

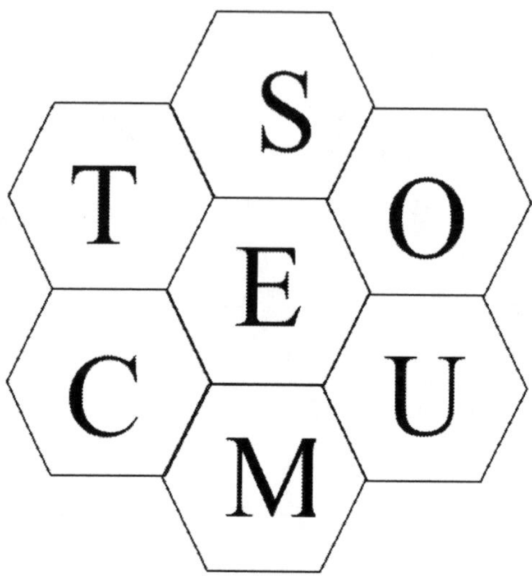

Use all the letters in the pangram to create a word from chapter 4. You can use letters multiple times. Write the word you made below.

Chapter 4 Word Scramble

Unscramble the following words.

Scrambled Word	**Unscrambled Word**
tearsaep	
dividnaliu	
sueis	
ninwiw	
gib cipetur	
cutomoes	

Answers

Chapter 4 Word Search Answers

T	C	R	G	E	C	O	N	F	L	I	C	T	S	S	G	F	K	L	H
H	A	S	R	A	T	T	E	Y	E	S	G	C	A	L	O	T	N	W	O
O	L	L	A	E	E	T	S	I	P	A	G	Y	S	I	T	L	E	S	C
U	M	I	T	T	T	F	K	D	X	O	P	L	O	S	U	A	W	F	O
T	T	F	E	I	B	W	I	B	I	L	T	M	A	T	I	U	O	N	N
C	W	Q	U	E	S	I	I	O	N	S	W	D	Q	E	E	D	T	I	V
O	R	T	B	A	M	U	G	V	E	E	P	I	O	N	T	I	A	W	E
M	S	T	A	T	E	M	E	P	T	F	I	A	P	A	P	V	I	A	R
E	Z	P	A	N	C	R	A	S	I	L	V	E	A	M	E	I	R	P	S
S	X	I	F	L	E	R	T	U	I	C	E	O	C	O	O	D	R	Z	A
I	X	I	R	C	A	O	E	H	C	S	T	G	T	N	P	N	O	W	T
R	V	I	H	T	A	S	K	P	H	E	X	U	O	D	T	I	L	L	I
R	B	S	E	U	V	G	Y	E	T	Y	B	E	R	J	Y	E	N	O	O
O	N	S	R	Y	R	E	S	P	O	I	S	S	U	E	T	I	O	N	N
R	M	E	L	T	H	N	U	T	F	U	B	G	I	C	J	B	V	K	M
E	W	N	Y	R	Y	J	I	L	V	J	B	H	M	U	R	R	O	R	Y
S	E	G	R	E	U	M	K	E	B	N	I	W	N	I	W	G	U	E	T
C	Y	D	I	A	L	O	G	U	E	Y	H	I	O	G	H	K	S	H	U

Chapter 4 Pangram Answer

Outcomes

Chapter 4 Word Scramble Answers

Unscrambled Word
separate
individual
issue
win win
big picture
outcomes

CHAPTER 5

Take Charge

"You will see it when you believe it."
-Wayne Dyer

Self-Awareness

Ivory and Avery were best friends. They were both biracial. Ivory had long wavey red hair and green eyes. Avery had long curly brown hair and brown eyes. Even though they were both of Caucasian and African ancestry, they appeared more Caucasian.

Ivory and Avery worked at a call center after school. They were both seventeen years old and were typical teenagers. The two also claimed to be able to spot a biracial person a mile away. According to them, this was because being biracial had enabled them to become human biracial radar detectors.

One day a new girl named Alice started working at the call center with them. She looked Caucasian and was dubbed "the new white girl." However, because Ivory and Avery were human biracial radar detectors, they knew differently.

A few weeks later, Ivory and Avery struck up a conversation about being biracial with Alice. Ivory then probed, "Are you biracial?" Alice was shocked and objected, "No. I'm just plain old white. Why would you ask me that?" Ivory smiled and pursued, "I just thought you were biracial. That's all." Alice had lily-white skin, freckles, brown eyes, and long, wavey, blond hair. To everyone else she looked Caucasian—but not to Avery and Ivory.

A week later, Avery, Ivory, and Alice had a shift at the call center together. Alice approached Avery and Ivory and told them a remarkable story. Alice divulged that after their conversation the week prior, she went home and told her mother about it. Her mother then started crying and revealed to Alice that her biological father was indeed of African descent. As the story went, Alice's mother had been dating two guys at the time of her pregnancy.

Alice's mother then told her biological father that she was pregnant, however, he refused to believe that the child was his. So, she then told the other man that the baby was his. Her mother was able to get away with the lie all of these years because Alice could pass as Caucasian, so no one ever questioned her paternity.

After being told the truth, Alice was shocked and felt as if she was falling down an identity crisis rabbit hole. Her whole life seemed like a lie. How did she not know? How could her mother have kept this secret from her? How was this happening to her?

After the shock wore off, Alice went from thinking she was Caucasian to knowing she was biracial. So, Alice started to embrace her African heritage. She submerged herself in her new found culture. She watched documentaries, read books, searched ancestry records, etc.

Alice had transformed from a plain caterpillar into a monarch butterfly. She had started sampling different types of music, eating different kinds of food, and trying out new fashion. Within a few months she had become a new person.

Consequently, Avery and Ivory had a new biracial friend. They had released Alice from the Matrix of lies that she was plugged into her entire life, and had given her a new identity and new life. Alice had now become self-aware and was able to embrace and honor all aspects of her ancestry.

As shocking as the story about Alice was, we are all guilty of living a life filled with a lack of awareness. However, unlike Alice, our lack of awareness may deal with internal issues as opposed to external issues. A lot of people actually walk around in a state of denial. They don't want to see the way things really are because it may be easier to live a lie than to deal with the truth.

Being self-aware allows one to know themselves; the good, the bad, and the ugly. So, what does it mean to be self-aware? For me, it means that one should be knowledgeable about themself. One should be aware of what makes them happy, sad, angry, agitated, etc. When you are aware of why you may feel and act in certain ways, when faced with certain situations, you may then be able to alter your reactions, thoughts, and behaviors to those situations.

One evening I was talking to a friend of mine Piper. She was telling me that she had been gaining weight. Piper blamed it on the fact that she had to sit down all day in front of a computer screen. She then communicated that she had recently gotten an exercise bike that she rode every day, however, she was not losing weight. As the conversation progressed, she talked about the fact that she ate chocolate every day and always had ice crem on hand. Piper then told me that she had baked cookies the day before and had consumed half of them. I was taken aback by Piper's inability to see that she was probably gaining weight because of what she was eating. I then asked, "Do you think you are gaining weight because of all of the sweets you are eating?" She then trumpeted, "If I wasn't sitting down all day at a desk, I would not be gaining weight!" I then replied, "But you are sitting down at a desk all day. So, maybe you should stop eating all of those sugary foods." She then uttered, "Hmmm."

Arguably, it was easier for Piper to be in denial about her eating habits than to face the truth. She had always been skinny as a child and young adult. However, after having two kids coupled with the aging process, she had started to put on weight. Piper may not have been self-aware enough to realize that her metabolism had slowed down. As a result of this, she was quite comfortable blaming her weight gain on a desk job instead of what she was putting in her body.

Certainly, a desk job does lead to weight gain for many individuals. However, if one can't do anything about a desk job because it is how they make a living, then one can change their diet and exercise routine. It is common knowledge that by increasing one's daily physical exercise and decreasing one's daily caloric intake, one may be able to maintain a healthy weight while having a desk job.

The quote at the beginning of the chapter is worth looking at when understanding self-awareness. As Wayne Dyer observed, "You'll see it when you believe it." So, when you start to delve in to why you react to certain situations the way you do, you'll begin to gain insight in to your reactions. Your journey of self-awareness will start to reveal why you express anger, fear, happiness, sorrow, etc., in regards to certain issues and situations. You will then begin to unmask yourself, which may lead to greater understanding of your reactions, feelings, and attitudes about various issues and situations.

Humor

Having a sense of humor is definitely helpful when becoming self-aware. Humor is a technique used in mediation to help lighten the mood. In the case of self-awareness, self-deprecating humor is often helpful. This is where you poke fun at yourself. For instance, if you are aware that you like cookies, you can imagine yourself being the cookie monster stuffing cookies in to your mouth. Another example could be, if you have a sibling that angers you, you could imagine that you are a cartoon character that bursts into flames at the sight of them.

Humor eases the tension in a situation through laughter. As the saying goes, "laughter is the best medicine." It is known that laughter relieves stress, boosts one's mood, and helps to diminish pain. So, why not try it when dealing with unraveling the fabric of self-awareness.

When I worked at a television station, I was the assistant to the VP of Production; his name was Hampton. My job was to do whatever needed to be done. One day our team was getting ready for a regional award show. My job was to locate a high-profile Hollywood director and lead him and his entourage to their seats. I was a bit nervous because I didn't know what he looked like. So, I asked Hampton to describe him to me. Hampton conveyed, "He's the guy with the two-hundred-dollar haircut." Not knowing what a two-hundred-dollar haircut looked like on a guy, I then inquired, "How much does your haircut cost?" Hampton chortled, "Ten dollars." We both burst out laughing and my nervousness melted away. It was hilarious because Hampton knew that he didn't have a high-end stylist at his disposal. He also knew that he just went to the discount hair place near to his house. As well, Hampton commented that his wife and kids would think he had lost his mind if he had ever gotten a two-hundred-dollar haircut. The fact that Hampton was self-aware enough to know that he had only ever gotten ten-dollar haircuts enabled him to make light of the situation and consequently eased my nervousness.

My intention for this chapter is for you to realize that learning about yourself does not have to be an excruciating process. Like I had said before, conversation coaching is not therapy. My main objective with coaching is to get you to better comprehend how you can best handle and deal with difficult conversations. So, in order to do that one must be able to understand and be aware of what makes one happy, sad, angry, agitated, etc. Just like I had said earlier, the only buttons that work on the conversational coaching remote are pause, play, and fast forward. Therefore, when dealing with self-awareness, one must press the pause button. The reason for this is because by pressing pause, you will be able to evaluate your reactions to certain issues or situations.

We can all learn to press the pause button with a little practice. For example, if you get anxious about speaking to your boss and you have a meeting with her in a few hours; just press the pause button in your mind. Once you have done this, think about why you get nervous. Maybe it's because you feel she will fire you if she thinks you are not doing a good job. Thus, by being self-aware about your anxiety, you can be better prepared to deal with the issue. So, if you have been doing your job to the best of your ability, then you will have nothing to be anxious about during your meeting. This realization may help to ease your anxiety during your meeting. Once you have figured out why you may be feeling anxious, you can press the play button in your mind and know that the meeting will go well because you would have nothing to worry about.

Self-Regulation

When I had moved to the Bahamas, I needed a new doctor. I just wanted to have someone that I could go to regularly in case I needed a check-up or had any health concerns. So, I asked around. Since a lot of my in-laws were in the health care profession, I asked them for a recommendation. I received a recommendation for Dr. Gray from one of them. At first, I was a bit hesitant because I always preferred to have a female doctor, however, I decided to overlook this because he was recommended to me. So, I went.

At the wellness visit, I was told to undress and put on the dreaded blue gown and wait for Dr. Gray. However, I still kept my undergarments on as I waited. After the visit was over, I left the office with a clean bill of health. "That wasn't so bad," I thought to myself as I drove home.

The following weekend, a family friend was having a party. So, of course I went. Whilst there, I happened to see Dr. Gray. Being social, I went over to him with some friends. I smiled and hummed, "Hey Dr. Gray, how have you been since I last saw you at your office a few days ago?" He smiled and declared, "Hey, I almost didn't recognize you with your clothes on." Instantly, my blood boiled with rage. I thought I would spontaneously combust from the anger and heat that coursed through my body. All I could hear was the sound of my heart beating as all other sounds faded into the background. My friends stood there muzzled in awkward silence. I felt like everything was moving in slow motion as I looked at him and walked away.

If there was ever a time in my life that I had to regulate my emotions—it was then. There he was, a family friend who had no regard for his insensitivity. In an alternate universe, I would have told him how rude he was. I would have told him how much of a pig he was. I would have told him how unprofessional he was. I may have even thrown the glass that I had been holding at him. However, I kept my cool and restrained myself because he was a well-respected physician and a family friend.

Undoubtedly, the first step to self-regulation is self-awareness. Once you are self-aware about what makes you happy, sad, angry, agitated, etc., you can then proceed on to regulating your responses to various issues and situations. Thus, when you become self-aware, you may invariably be able to exert self-control when dealing with difficult conversations and issues.

If Piper was able to become self-aware about her consumption of excessive calories, she would then be able to self-regulate her food choices. For instance, Piper may then start to make different choices at the grocery store. Instead of buying chocolate, she could buy dried fruit. Instead of buying ice cream, she could buy low-fat yogurt. Instead of baking cookies, she could bake fruit. So, by becoming aware of her choices, she could start to self-regulate by making different decisions when it comes to selecting and curating her food.

Positivity

As a marketing specialist, I worked with a group of women. There were seven of us. A few months after I started working at the office, another female named Ocean-Rae was hired. I instantly liked her. We were the same age, and her birthday was the day before mine. We all had our own schedules. Some days, I worked alone; if I had to work on the weekends.

One weekend however, I happened to be working with my co-worker Jane. A few hours in to our day, Jane started talking about Ocean-Rae. She proceeded to trash Ocean-Rae's personality and claimed that she was a train wreck. I refused to engage her and just continued working. When she was finished, I turned to her and inquired, "Do you feel better about your life now that you've talked about Ocean-Rae?" She just glared at me and scowled, "Her life's a disaster. That's all I'm saying."

Needless to say, the next time I worked with Ocean-Rae, I told her that Jane had trashed her and was not to be trusted. I also told her to watch what she said around Jane because she was a horrible gossip. Ocean-Rae just sat there with a hurt look on her face as I continued to report what had been said.

To my amazement, Ocean-Rae looked at me and asserted, "I refuse to say anything negative about anyone." I couldn't believe it. Ocean-Rae was a saint. Never in my entire life had I met someone who refused to say anything negative about anyone; especially someone who had assassinated their character. I was floored as I stood there in utter disbelief. From that day forward I admired Ocean-Rae's super human ability to exert self-regulation when faced with a difficult situation. My eyes had been opened to the new world of self-regulation when faced with difficult issues.

Ocean-Rae's ability to maintain a positive attitude when faced with adversity was refreshing. In mediation, one is also encouraged to be positive when faced with difficulties as well. However, as we all know, it is often difficult to be positive when faced with tough issues. Ultimately, it is simply a decision one must consciously make and stick to. If one holds firm to the fact that they will be positive when faced with difficult issues, then they will probably be able to work through any complications that may arise when dealing with tough situations.

On the contrary, if one remains negative, they may want to throw in the towel and give up when faced with difficulties. Thus, the Pygmalion effect will appear one way or the other. So, why not be positive, which may very well result in a favorable outcome when faced with tough issues. So, the next time you're faced with a negative situation, simply think to yourself—what would Ocean-Rae do (WWORD)?

Self-Determination

Bella was a relative of my former husband. One day, we were talking about a doctor's visit she had recently had. At the time, Bella was in medical school and was home for the summer. She had been to the doctor the week prior because she had a small rash. She said that she was told to change in to the dreaded blue gown and wait for the doctor. Bella then said that while she was waiting, she saw the paperwork that needed to be filled out sitting on the counter. Bella then observed that her visit didn't entail her getting undressed. Before she could get dressed, the doctor had entered the examination room. He proceeded to perform a physical on her. She was frozen and didn't know what to do because he was a family friend. Bella then told me that she had told her father about the incident. However, he had told her that she was just making a big deal about it.

Justifiably, the incident had left her distraught and upset. I looked at her and questioned, "Which doctor was it?" She then replied, "Dr. Gray." My blood turned to molten lava at the sound of his name. I was outraged that he had done this to her. How dare he! I then recounted the incident at the party to her. Bella then turned to me and inquired, "Will you come to his office with me? I want to tell him how I feel about what he did." Without hesitation I answered, "When do you want me to pick you up?"

The next day, Bella and I descended upon Dr. Gray's office with an agenda to make things right. Bella walked up to him and confronted him about his misconduct. She told him that she knew what he had done was wrong. He knew she was right, as he was fully aware that she was a medical student. He did not admit to any wrongdoing but he knew that she had a right to be angry at him, as he stood there with shame stamped on his forehead. When she had finished speaking her truth, we proudly walked out of there and never looked back.

Bella's self-determination allowed her to stand up for her beliefs. She knew what Dr. Gray had done was inappropriate, even though her father had wanted to sweep it under the rug because he didn't want to cause problems with his friend and colleague. I was proud of her for confronting Dr. Gray. This is because it may have caused him to re-evaluate his behavior. Furthermore, Bella's actions may have even prevented other women from being mistreated by Dr. Gray. All in all, Bella was a hero in my eyes.

Self-determination is when a person takes control of their own life. Self-determined individuals take matters into their own hands. Ultimately, this is what Bella had done. She had taken control of her situation and confronted Dr. Gray—the person she had an issue with. When one is self-determined they are in the driver's seat and in control of their life.

Hence, when one has become self-aware, one will be able to have the ability to understand what issues trigger various feelings within oneself that can cause them to react in certain ways to various issues and situations. One can then better understand how they can react or regulate themselves in certain situations or when dealing with various issues. Moreover, when one has honed the ability to self-regulate, one can move on to the process of self-determination. Thus, they would then be equipped with the tools of self-awareness and self-regulation, which will allow them to ultimately control their reactions to various issues and situations.

Internal Locus of Control

In leadership, there is a concept called internal locus of control. As purported by DuBrin (2013) "People with an internal locus of control believe that they are the prime mover behind events" (p.50). They basically feel that their circumstances are a direct result of their actions. They believe that their lives are controlled by internal factors and their own choices and decisions. In contrast, people with an external locus of control believe that their lives are controlled by external factors such as fate, luck, chance, etc.

In my mind, the concepts of internal locus of control and self-determination are linked. This is because self-determined individuals are in control of their lives. Hence, they must be driven by their internal locus of control. Therefore, once one starts to realize that they are in control of their lives, they may be propelled to make choices and decisions that reflect the type of life they want for themselves.

When I worked as a marketing specialist, I was making a pretty good income. I was quite content with my salary and bonuses that I was receiving. However, one day I got wind that a co-worker of mine—Cassi—was getting paid more than I was. I couldn't understand why she would be paid more than I was since we were both doing the same job. In fact, my educational requirements far exceeded that of hers. I was outraged and confused.

Driven by my belief in the concept of an internal locus of control, I picked up the phone and called my boss. I told him that I needed a 25% pay increase. I didn't mention that I knew Cassi made more money than I did. He was taken aback by my request. However, he told me that he would call me back. An hour later my phone rang. My boss had called me back and had agreed to give me a 12.5% raise. He also said that I would receive another raise based on my performance review at the end of the year. I thanked him for the raise and hung up the phone.

A few days later, my friend Grace called me. I told her that I had received a raise and then went into the details of how it had transpired. She was shocked that I had not gotten fired because of my outlandish request. I was surprised by her reaction. Grace said that people never strong arm their bosses. Everyone she knew usually just waited patiently until they got their annual reviews before they even considered asking for a raise. I then protested, "How would you get what you want if you don't ask for it?" Radio silence filled the phone line. Grace then complied, "True." At the end of the day, I had the gusto to go after what I wanted—a raise—and I got it.

Interestingly, the thing that I am most proud of being self-determined about does not involve money or material wealth. I am most proud of my ability to have raised a child without using violence. For me, this is a huge accomplishment. Primarily because I grew up in a culture where abuse and violence were rampant. Everyone used violence to discipline their children. Personally, I believe that some parents disguised the abuse they subjected their children to by labeling it as discipline. This may have enabled them to lie to themselves and others about the abuse that went on in their homes. By doing this, they could shield themselves from the ramifications that abusers are faced with in society; such as jail. I was even told by a relative that people beat their children as a way to relieve their stress. Another adult relative, who had been the recipient of abuse, had even whispered to me, "You never call the police on family." I then responded, "If anyone is being abused, they should call the police." As an adult, I know that abuse is not discipline.

So, when my child was born, I knew that I would not use violence to raise her. Instead, I used love and words. I found alternatives to violence such as time out, taking away privileges, groundings, etc. By believing that I possessed an internal locus of control, I was able to break the cycle of violence that had plagued people from my cultural background. I am so glad that I was able to achieve my goal of not using violence to discipline my child. Unquestionably, it is my greatest accomplishment and the thing that I am most proud of.

Fundamentally, the concepts of self-awareness, self-regulation, and self-determination will prepare one to take charge of their life. These three concepts will enable one to control their reactions when faced with difficult situations or issues. By utilizing humor and remaining positive, one will also be able to embark on the road to dealing with tough issues. Furthermore, these concepts and techniques will enable one to handle difficult conversations about race, gender, and violence when they arise or are brought to their attention.

Exercise 1

Write about a time that you became self-aware about something.

Exercise 2

Write about a time that you were able to self-regulate yourself.

Exercise 3

Visualize ***what you look like when you are determined to do something.*** You can draw a picture in the box if you want or you can simply visualize it in your mind's eye.

Chapter 5 Word Search

C	A	R	G	E	N	T	I	R	A	O	B	C	S	S	L	P	K	L	T
N	S	E	R	N	T	T	A	B	U	O	G	O	A	J	O	Y	N	W	O
O	T	L	A	O	E	T	H	O	M	I	L	N	G	S	V	I	E	S	L
I	A	I	T	I	T	L	I	U	T	E	N	V	I	G	E	L	W	F	E
T	T	G	E	T	B	W	I	B	M	L	T	T	A	D	I	S	O	N	R
A	W	I	U	A	S	T	R	A	S	O	I	R	Q	U	E	S	T	I	A
N	R	O	B	L	M	U	H	V	Q	V	R	S	O	V	T	E	A	W	N
I	S	N	A	U	E	P	E	N	I	F	A	I	T	H	P	I	I	A	P
M	Z	P	A	G	C	R	E	A	T	O	R	L	A	M	E	M	R	O	E
R	X	I	S	E	L	F	A	W	A	R	E	N	E	S	S	I	S	Z	F
E	C	L	G	R	F	E	R	H	C	S	A	R	O	H	P	I	O	W	D
T	V	I	H	F	D	F	T	P	H	E	X	U	N	L	T	T	L	L	M
E	B	E	L	L	E	F	Y	E	T	Y	B	E	V	I	Y	E	N	O	V
D	N	T	K	E	B	H	C	F	G	V	X	R	V	I	R	R	O	R	F
F	M	Y	O	S	S	T	A	T	E	M	E	I	T	C	J	B	V	K	R
L	A	L	M	D	I	A	L	O	G	U	T	H	S	I	R	W	O	R	Y
E	E	G	R	E	U	M	K	E	B	Y	D	I	A	B	O	G	U	E	T
S	C	C	E	P	T	L	O	R	T	N	O	C	F	O	S	U	C	O	L

Words To Find		
SELF AWARENESS	SELF DETERMINATION	POSITIVITY
SELF REGULATION	LOCUS OF CONTROL	HUMOR

Chapter 5 Pangram

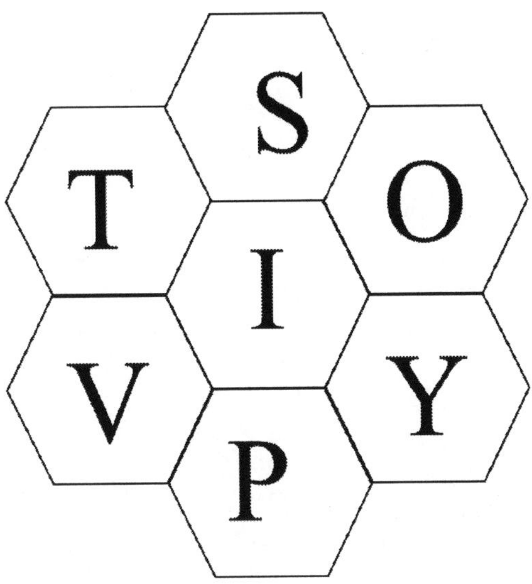

Use all the letters in the pangram to create a word from chapter 5. You can use letters multiple times. Write the word you made below.

____

Chapter 5 Word Scramble

Unscramble the following words.

Scrambled Word	Unscrambled Word
fels-nearwases	
elfs-laguretnoi	
lefs-termindetanio	
rumoh	
sitviptoyi	
Terminal solcu fo tonrolc	

Answers

Chapter 5 Word Find Answers

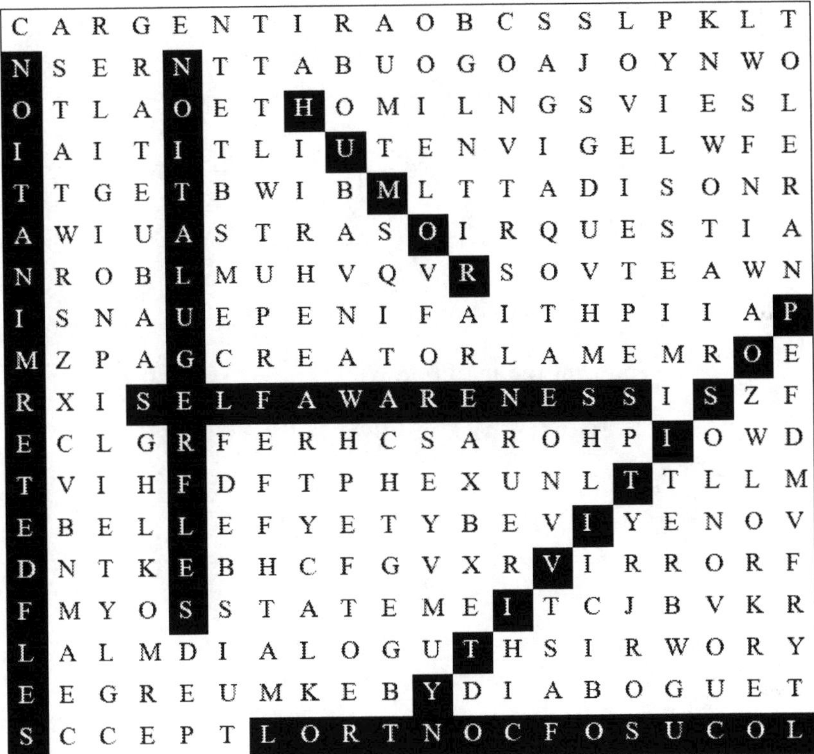

Chapter 5 Pangram Answer

Positivity

Chapter 5 Word Scramble Answers

Unscrambled Word
self-awareness
self-regulation
self-determination
humor
positivity
internal locus of control

CHAPTER 6

Unplug

"Our intention creates reality."
-Wayne Dyer

Our Senses

When I was eight years old, my class went on a school trip to a conservation area on the outskirts of Toronto, Canada. Upon arrival to the conservation area, everyone was paired up with a partner. We were given a map and a compass and told to find our way back to the building where we would be leaving from to go back to school.

I was paired with Parker. We were both clueless about how to use the compass. This may have been because neither one of us had been listening to the teacher when she was explaining how to use the compass.

Needless to say, Parker and I got lost in the woods. We roamed around aimlessly. We eventually got thirsty and drank water from the pond, which we later found out could make us sick. When we finally managed to get back to the building, we saw the school bus driving off in the distance. I guess a teacher spotted us, because the bus came back to collect us.

When I think back to the day at the conservation area, I am particularly struck by the fact that one can hear but not listen. This is what some would call selective hearing. Since we can't turn off our hearing, we often choose to tune others out. As can be seen from my adventure at the conservation area, it is a skill that even a child can master.

Fundamentally, this is what people who meditate do. Meditators, like everyone else, cannot turn off their minds, so they selectively dismiss the thoughts that enter their minds. They choose to view thoughts as waves of perception that come and go. They simply swipe the thoughts out of their minds the same way you would swipe an image on your phone. They choose not to go deep into any thought that may enter their mind while focusing on their breathing.

Subsequently, one can even tune out smells. As we all know, you cannot turn off your sense of smell. However, when a smell is all around us, we get used to the scent and can no longer smell it because our nose has adapted to the smell. Incidentally, this is what some refer to as being "nose blind." We have all experienced this phenomenon before. If you have ever cooked a meal for a dinner party, your sense of smell would have adapted to the scent of the food and you would have become "nose blind" to it. On the other hand, upon arrival, your guests may have commented on how good the food smelled.

Incidentally, the fact that our senses can adapt to our surrounding is great. Primarily because we can use this information to help us deal with anxiety that often arises when one is faced with difficult conversations. By learning to relax when faced with difficult conversations, you will be able to fully engage with the issues at hand.

Change

Change is something that occurs in life. In fact, it occurs in all aspects of life. According to Kreitner and Kinicki (2013) "Lewin developed a three-stage model of planned change that explained how to initiate, manage, and stabilize the change process" (p. 536). This is known as Lewin's Change Model. The model encapsulates three stages of change: unfreezing, changing, and refreezing.

I first encountered Lewin's Change Model in my management studies; as organizations use it to change the attitudes and behaviors of their employees in regards to new processes and procedures. However, I quickly realized that this model can be utilized by individuals to change their attitudes and behaviors in regards to a variety of issues.

Unfreezing is the first step in which individuals have to be motivated to want to change. Thus, once one wants to change their old patterns, they can then start to unfreeze their attitudes and be open to new ideas and new ways of thinking about issues and situations.

Change is the second step which involves learning new procedures or behaviors. So, it is necessary for one to take the time to acquire the necessary skills and behaviors that will facilitate change. Once learned, one is on their way to the final stage of the change process.

Refreezing is the third and final step of the change process. This is where one refreezes the new attitudes and behavior that have been developed as a result of the change process. Once the new behaviors and attitudes have been learned and incorporated in to the normal way of doing things, the change process would have been completed successfully. Ultimately, the goal of the change process is to create new habits via the new procedures and attitudes.

Lewin's change process can be seen during the covid pandemic. For instance, before the pandemic, most individuals went to their office to work. However, due to the outbreak, a lot of individuals had to adapt to working from home. At first, some people were resistant to the change. Nevertheless, they had to unfreeze their old views about working in an office. They also had to learn new processes and procedures for working from home, such as video conferencing and utilizing various software. Moreover, once everyone acquired the new skills, they were then able to incorporate them in to their daily lives. Individuals were then able to refreeze their new attitudes and behaviors, ultimately making their new way of working from home a habit.

So, how is Lewin's change model going to help you deal with difficult issues and assist you with engaging in difficult conversations? Well, you can use it to help you learn how to relax. You can learn to subside anxiety and nervousness by learning to calm yourself before embarking on difficult conversations.

The first stage of unfreezing is already occurring. This is because you are reading this book which is about having difficult conversations. Therefore, you are demonstrating that you are motivated to want to change and desire to learn new skills. Take a moment and give yourself a pat on the back for that.

The second stage of change is occurring right now. This is due to the fact that you are taking the time to acquire the necessary skills and behaviors to facilitate relaxing before embarking on difficult conversations. Subsequently, this will be achieved via a few relaxation exercises that I have created. Simply read over the exercises and then actually do each of the relaxation exercises. Write down any thoughts, feelings, and observations you may have after doing each exercise in the space provided.

Relaxation Exercise 1: Shaking

Stand up and shake out your hands.

Next, shake out your arms.

Then, shake out your shoulders.

Continue shaking out your hands, arms, and shoulders while bending your knees.

After you have done this for a minute, stop.

Stand still.

Now, observe the tingling sensation in your body.

****

What thoughts, feelings, or observations do you have about the relaxation exercise?

Relaxation Exercise 2: Dandelion

Pick up a pen and hold it in your hand.

Now, imagine you are holding a dandelion.

Hold the dandelion a few inches from your face.

Take a deep breath in.

Hold it for 3 seconds.

Now, blow out deeply and imagine that you are blowing the seeds off of your dandelion.

Take another deep breath in.

Hold it for 3 seconds.

Now, blow out deeply and imagine that you are blowing some more seeds off of your dandelion.

Take another long deep breath in.

Hold it for 3 seconds.

Now, blow out deeply and imagine that you are blowing the remaining seeds off of your dandelion.

Now, breathe normally and observe how relaxed you feel.

****

What thoughts, feelings, or observations do you have about the relaxation exercise?

Relaxation Exercise 3: Melting

Imagine that you are in the arctic.

The cold wind is blowing on your face.

You are feeling very cold.

Now, the sun has come out.

It is warming your face.

You start to feel warm.

The sun is very hot.

It starts to melt the stress away from your body.

The stress starts to melt away from the top of your head.

The stress melts away from your neck.

The stress melts away from your arms, hands, and fingers.

The stress melts away from your upper back and lower back.

The stress melts away from your legs.

The stress melts away from your feet.

Now, observe how relaxed you feel.

****

What thoughts, feelings, or observations do you have about the relaxation exercise?

Now that you have done all of the relaxation exercises, you are on your way to the third and final step of refreezing your new attitudes and behaviors. Pick one of the exercises and do it regularly. The more you do it, the more relaxed you will become when faced with difficult issues. It will be a very useful habit to have when faced with tough issues.

My intention for this chapter is for you to learn at least one relaxation technique. This will allow you to utilize the technique when embarking on difficult conversations. By simply learning how to relax, you would be able to focus on the issues at hand and think more clearly about the topics that are being discussed.

The Wayne Dyer quote at the beginning of the chapter, "Our intention creates reality," is quite fitting for this chapter. That is because if you intend on dealing with difficult issues with a calm state of mind, then you will. Hence, by simply focusing on being relaxed whilst engaged in a difficult conversation, you will be able to effectively deal with the issues. When you are able to subdue anxiety and nervousness, you will be able to create a new reality for yourself.

Small Victories

Consider the skill of learning to relax as a small victory for yourself. In mediation, the concept of small victories is used to celebrate any achievement that one makes that aligns with one's intentions. Small victories give us a boost of confidence. It allows us to know that we are capable of tiny wins. Thus, if we are capable of small victories, then we are also capable of big victories as well. Therefore, if you are capable of relaxing before embarking on a difficult conversation, just chalk it up to being the little win before you achieve the big win of tackling the difficult issue via dialogue.

Once you are able to unplug and relax, you will feel like a new person. It may be like a scene from *The Matrix*— when Neo unplugged from the Matrix, only to look around and see that everyone else was still plugged in. If you can unplug and relax, you will be able to see the issues more clearly. You may even be able to tackle tough issues and get the desired outcome that you want to achieve.

Here are some other ways to relax:

1. Birdwatching videos
2. Exercise
3. Observing nature

Exercise 1

List the things ***you do*** to relax.

1.

2.

3.

4.

5.

6.

7.

8.

9.

10.

Exercise 2

List the things ***you can do*** to relax.

1.

2.

3.

4.

5.

6.

7.

8.

9.

10.

Exercise 3

Visualize ***what you look like*** when you are relaxed. You can draw a picture in the box if you want or you can simply visualize it in your mind's eye.

Chapter 6 Word Search

S	A	C	G	E	N	T	P	M	A	O	B	C	S	S	C	H	K	L	C
A	M	O	R	A	T	T	A	B	U	O	G	C	A	B	O	Y	N	O	O
T	T	A	A	E	E	T	S	O	M	I	L	H	U	I	N	I	M	Y	L
E	A	F	L	T	T	L	I	D	T	E	N	A	E	T	V	M	W	O	E
P	T	L	E	L	B	W	I	B	I	W	T	N	N	D	U	I	O	T	P
N	W	I	U	E	V	L	R	A	R	I	W	G	D	N	R	R	T	S	I
O	R	C	B	G	E	I	D	E	R	N	P	E	I	V	E	T	E	T	N
I	S	T	A	T	E	S	C	N	T	W	A	S	R	L	A	E	I	A	D
T	Z	O	A	N	C	T	E	T	T	I	A	L	A	M	V	N	R	P	I
A	X	G	S	T	A	S	K	M	O	T	T	X	C	U	I	I	R	Y	V
S	C	U	G	K	F	E	R	H	I	R	A	R	H	H	O	S	O	M	E
R	V	E	H	I	D	F	T	O	H	L	I	U	P	L	L	T	L	E	Z
E	B	K	L	K	E	E	Z	E	E	R	F	E	R	J	E	E	N	N	E
V	N	T	K	Y	M	I	R	R	O	R	X	R	S	I	N	R	O	T	E
N	M	Y	P	E	R	C	E	P	T	I	O	N	E	C	C	B	V	K	R
O	A	T	D	S	T	Y	T	E	M	E	N	T	S	I	E	W	O	R	F
C	E	N	O	I	S	H	A	K	I	N	G	I	A	B	O	G	U	E	N
A	F	R	T	E	D	I	S	S	U	E	N	L	I	G	T	E	N	H	U

Words To Find		
UNFREEZE	CHANGES	REFREEZE
RELAX	SHAKING	SMALL VICTORIES

Chapter 6 Pangram

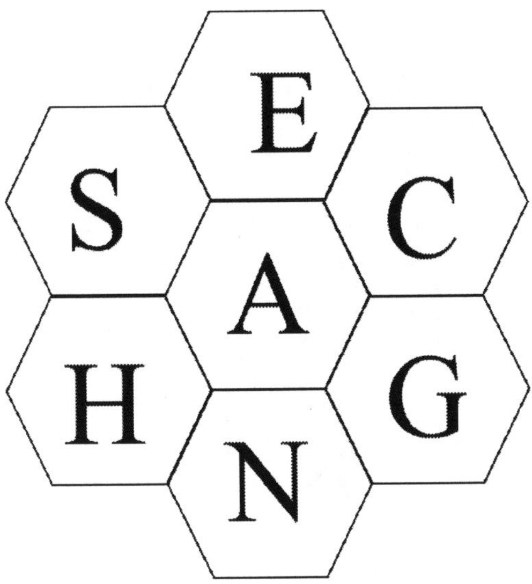

Use all the letters in the pangram to create a word from chapter 6. You can use letters multiple times. Write the word you made below.

____

Chapter 6 Word Scramble

Unscramble the following words.

Scrambled Word	Unscrambled Word
runfrezee	
shagnec	
frezeere	
larex	
kingsha	
malls storieciv	

Answers

Chapter 6 Word Search Answers

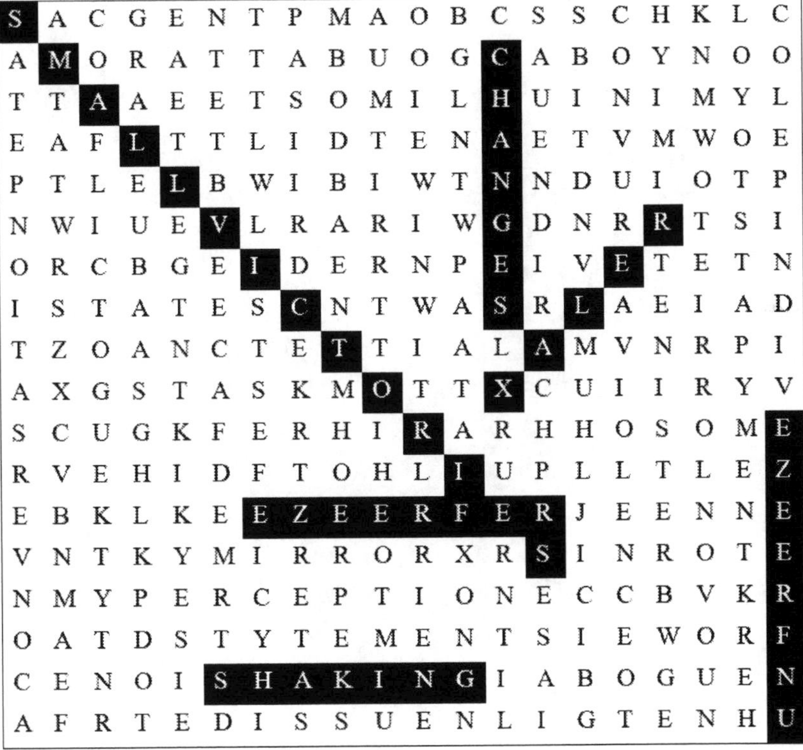

Chapter 6 Pangram Answer

Changes

Chapter 6 Word Scramble Answers

Unscrambled Word
unfreeze
changes
refreeze
relax
shaking
small victories

CHAPTER 7

Spark A CALM Dialogue

"It's never crowded along the extra mile."
-Wayne Dyer

Words Over Fists

When I was in university, I was dating Xander. One day we were at a pool party with a group of friends and acquaintances. I was wading around in the pool when Logan—one of Xander's friends—came over. I had met him a few times and was aware that he had a girlfriend. Even though we were the same age, he always struck me as an old soul and reminded me of someone's uncle. So, I never really paid much attention to him.

Logan proceeded to sit down at the edge of the pool. He then started complimenting me. I smiled and looked around and scanned the premises for Xander. I spotted him with a group of people laughing and having a good time. Logan leaned forward, grabbed my hand, and professed, "I am so attracted to you. I wish you were my girlfriend." Shocked and confused I gasped, "Let go of me." I managed to pull away from him and got out of the pool.

When I was able to get Xander alone, I told him what had happened. Without saying a word, he marched over to Logan and confronted him. Logan looked at him and denied it. Logan then squawked, "Xander, who are you going to believe; me or that stupid girl?" In an instant, Xander curled his fist and punched Logan in the mouth.

At the time it seemed to be the most appropriate response. However, now that I look back on the incident, I wonder if it could have been handled differently. If I had known how to use my voice effectively, I would have been able to show Logan the error of his ways via the CALM Dialogue.

The CALM Dialogue

We have finally arrived at the chapter about the CALM Dialogue. The CALM Dialogue's 4-step process will enable anyone to embark on difficult conversations pertaining to race, gender, and violence. The CALM in the CALM Dialogue is an acronym. Therefore, the letters in the word CALM each stand for something. Now you will be able to find out what each letter stands for, as well as, how each concept should be used. So, let's get started.

C Stands for Conversation Begins with an I-Statement

The C in the CALM Acronym stands for—Conversation begins with an I-Statement. I-Statements describe how you are feeling. Therefore, when you embark on a difficult conversation, you would begin the conversation with the phrase "I feel." The I-Statement usually lets the other person know how you are feeling. So, you would simply identify how you are feeling and phrase it using an I-Statement.

Being self-aware will allow you to effectively come up with an I-Statement. Remember that when you are self-aware, you will be able to identify what makes you feel happy, sad, angry, agitated, etc. Therefore, by being able to identify your emotions, you will be able to compose an I-Statement based on your feelings.

Below is a list of "I feel" phrases to help you get familiarized with using I-Statements.

"I Feel" Phrases:

1. I feel angry because I got yelled at.
2. I feel frustrated because I was ignored.
3. I feel sad because my feelings were hurt.
4. I feel agitated because I was tricked.
5. I feel happy about the plan.
6. I feel scared because I don't know what the future holds.
7. I feel betrayed because of all the lies I have been told.
8. I feel embarrassed because I fell.
9. I feel anxious because we are not in agreement.
10. I feel nervous talking about this issue.

I-Statements can also be in the form of an "I am" phrase. So, you can just make a statement about an observation that you are having and say it using an "I am" phrase.

Below are some "I am" phrases to help you get started with using I-Statements.

"I Am" phrases:

1. I am glad that we talked.
2. I am going to take your advice.
3. I am thinking about doing that.
4. I am going to go there later.
5. I am surprised to hear you say that.
6. I am happy to hear that.
7. I am going to remember that.
8. I am thrilled about your decision.
9. I am up for the challenge.
10. I am onboard with the decision.

An I-Statement can also just be a general response or statement about the topic. All you have to do is use "I" in the sentence to let the other person know that you are conveying your comments and sentiments about the discussion. Using "I" in a sentence lets the other person know that you are actively participating in the conversation.

Below are some examples of I-Statements that use the word "I" to help you get started with using I-Statements.

"I" phrases:

1. I guess that could be a possibility.
2. I can understand the reason that happened.
3. I have been following the news as well.
4. I have heard that argument before.
5. I think you have a point.
6. I would like to hear more about that issue.
7. I like that group too.
8. I sympathize with that cause.

9. I can do that now.
10. I want things to change as well.

Without a doubt, you will need to self-regulate whilst having a difficult conversation. For example, if you know the person is a liar, you will have to refrain from using an accusatory statement. You will have to channel your energy in to creating a habit of using I-Statements to identify your feelings. So, you could say, "I am frustrated because you lied to me," instead of, "You're a liar!" As you can see the last statement will cause the person to become defensive and doesn't identify how you feel. In the end, I-Statements are more effective than accusatory statements when communicating with others.

Self-determination also plays a role in the first step of the CALM Dialogue. This is because you will have to take control of the situation by initiating a CALM Dialogue about the tough issues that you wish to discuss. Thus, by embarking on a CALM Dialogue, you will ultimately be able to take matters in to your own hands. Additionally, you will be able to delve in to issues that need to be discussed so that you can move forward or beyond the present situation. All in all, using the CALM Dialogue may lead to higher awareness and greater understanding about the issues at hand.

A Stands for Ask Questions

The A in the CALM acronym stands for—Ask questions. In this step, you would simply ask the person you are talking to a question about the issue at hand. For example, you could inquire, "How did that happen?" Remember, open-ended questions are the best questions to ask someone when you are trying to gain understanding about a particular situation. This is because it allows the speaker to tell their narrative at length.

Below is a list of open-ended questions to help you get started with asking questions during a difficult discussion.

Open-ended question:

1. Why is that?
2. What do you think?
3. Do you agree?

4. How should we do this?
5. Where is the best location for that?
6. Is there a better way?
7. What ideas did you have?
8. When would be a good day to do that?
9. What do you want to discuss first?
10. Who should we invite?

L Stands for Listen Carefully

The L in the CALM acronym stands for—Listen carefully. This means that you should listen empathetically to understand the other person. Therefore, after you ask the person a question, you would need to listen to their response carefully to truly comprehend the situation. Remember this means that you need to listen without interrupting them. It might be helpful to put an invisible bubble in your mouth when the other person is talking.

It might actually be helpful if you practiced listening carefully to other people before you embark on a difficult conversation. So, the next time you talk to someone, try to listen to them fully without interrupting. If you find yourself starting to interrupt, just put a bubble in your mouth. By practicing to refrain yourself from interrupting, you will be well prepared to listen carefully when having difficult conversations.

Below are a few practice exercises you can use when you are practicing how to be a better listener. Simply decide when you want to practice listening and arrange a meeting or visit with someone. Whilst talking, practice your listening skills and keep track of how many times you interrupted the person during the course of the conversation. Hopefully the number of times you interrupt a someone will decrease with each practice session. Once you have achieved the goal of not interrupting a person at all during the course of a conversation, you should give yourself a gold star.

First Practice for Listening Carefully

1. Person's name: ______________________________
2. Topic discussed: ______________________________
3. Numberoftimesyouinterrupted: ______________________________

Second Practice for Listening Carefully

1. Person's name: ______________________________
2. Topic discussed: ______________________________
3. Number of times you interrupted: ________________

Third Practice for Listening Carefully

1. Person's name: ______________________________
2. Topic discussed: ______________________________
3. Numberoftimesyouinterrupted:________________

M Stands for Mirror Responses with A You-Statement

The M in the CALM acronym stands for—Mirror response with a You-Statement. After you have empathetically listened to what the other person had to say, you would then mirror or repeat what they said using a You-Statement. A You-Statement in this regard is really a reflective statement. This is because you would paraphrase or restate what the other person said using a You-Statement. A reflective statement ensures that you understand the other person's message. It also enables the other person to clarify their message in the event that there is a misunderstanding.

The concept of reframing will also come in handy with mirroring a response with a You-Statement. For instance, this may be the case when the other person uses undesirable language when speaking. You can simply rephrase their words to make their statement more appealing when composing your You-Statement. This may help to de-escalate a heated discussion; as cooler heads will prevail when dealing with difficult conversations.

Conceptually, You-Statements are basically statements coupled with the word "you." You-Statements are not accusatory statements. So, they are not statements that attack the other person's character. Therefore, one would not say something that attacks the character of the other person like, "You are a thief!" Instead, one would restrain themselves and say something like, "So, you are saying that you did not take my name off of the report that we worked on together when you submitted it." On the whole, reframing a sentence into one that is more appealing to the other person will lead to better communication pertaining to difficult conversations.

Below is a list of You-Statements to help you get started with using You-Statements.

You-Statements:

1. Thank you for apologizing.
2. You are right, they should not have removed the comment box.
3. So, what you said is that the price has increased from last year.
4. You are correct, I do approve of that decision.
5. I can understand that you are upset because no one has responded yet.
6. You were right about visiting the facility yesterday.
7. So, you do agree with the decision.
8. If you are going there, please call first and make an appointment.
9. You can collect the paperwork tomorrow.
10. You should write your goals down.

How to Use the CALM Dialogue

Congratulations! You now know how to use the four steps in the CALM Dialogue. Consequently, you can use the steps interchangeably, so that the conversation flows naturally. This means that you do not have to always use the steps in order. Sometimes you might have a question you may want to ask. Sometimes you might want to chime in with an I-Statement. Therefore, it is up to you to use your judgement when you are having a difficult conversation as to what step to use next.

C-Conversation begins with an I-Statement
A-Ask questions
L-Listen carefully
M-Mirror response with a You-Statement

Below are three sample conversations about race, gender, and violence. I have created these conversations to demonstrate how the CALM Dialogue could be used to engage in a difficult conversation. As you read the samples over, you will see how the CALM Dialogue is used to structure the conversation in order to keep it moving forward. The ultimate goal of the CALM Dialogue is to attain a win/win outcome.

CALM Dialogue Race Scenario
Scenario Details

Austin and Perry are two Caucasian males. They were both born and raised in Kansas. As well, they both grew up in working class families. Austin loves to travel. So, as soon as he graduated high school, he started traveling to different countries. Visiting China was one of his favorite memories. Perry, on the other hand, prefers to travel domestically. He loves going to different states and looking at historical landmarks. They are both in their twenties now. One day they were hanging out at Austin's house when they had the following conversation.

Conversation begins with an I-Statement
Perry: I've been watching the news lately. Have you?

Ask questions
***Austin**: Yes. I watch it now and then. Why?*

Listen carefully
Perry: A lot of Asians have been getting attacked lately.
***Austin**: I've heard. I think it's awful.*

Mirror response with a You-Statement
Perry: You think it's awful. I think they're responsible for the world's problems.
***Austin**: What? You feel that they're the cause of our problems? These are American citizens. They are human beings. They are not to blame because they are suffering too. I am very surprised to hear you say that, Perry. Can you honestly think that Asian Americans or Asians anywhere in the world are the cause of our problems?*

Conversation begins with an I-Statement
Perry: Yes, I can! They created the virus that started this pandemic.

Ask questions
***Austin**: Wait a minute. You think all Asians are responsible for the pandemic? Even if a virus was leaked from a lab, it does not make all Asians responsible.*

That could have happened anywhere. It doesn't make it the fault of the Asian race. You have got to separate the individuals from the issue. The issue is the virus and the individuals are the people of Asian descent. You need to focus on the issue of the virus. In that case, the individuals are the government officials that mishandled the situation; not the Asian race. Don't you agree?

Listen carefully
Perry: I feel angry about the situation. I just want to blame someone. Why won't you just shut up and let me blame them?

Mirror response with a You-Statement
***Austin**: The reason that I won't let you blame innocent people is because they shouldn't be blamed for something they didn't do. If you want to assign blame, then you should place the blame on the government officials that mishandled the situation. Don't misplace your anger on the innocent Asian people.*

Conversation begins with an I-Statement
Perry: I guess you're right. I just needed to talk to someone about how I was feeling.
***Austin**: I'm glad that you talked to me about it.*
Perry: Me too.

CALM Dialogue Outcome

Austin was able to persuade Perry to see things from a different perspective. This was because he had the ability to separate the Asian people from the Pandemic. By separating the individuals from the issue, Austin was able to explain to Perry that the Asian race was not responsible for the Pandemic. When you are able to change someone's perspective, it may very well change their worldview.

CALM Dialogue Gender Scenario
Scenario Details

Aspen and Delta are Upper-level managers for a large corporation. They have been interviewing candidates for a senior level marketing position. The person would have to work extra hours and have the ability to travel occasionally. The two most qualified people for the position are Robin and Stanley. As they were making their decision, they had the following conversation.

Conversation begins with an I-Statement
Aspen: Well, I think Robin is the better candidate.

Ask questions
***Delta**: Why?*

Listen carefully
Aspen: Well, she's motivated and has a great work ethic. She is also a people person and has scored well on all of her performance reviews.

Mirror response with a You-Statement
***Delta**: I can hear that you think she's the most qualified. However, she just got married. Don't you think that would affect her performance? She may have done well on her performance reviews before, but what if she wants to start a family?*

Conversation begins with an I-Statement
Aspen: I'm surprised to hear you say that. Delta, what does her marital status have to do with her work performance? She applied for the position and she's qualified for the job. That's all that matters. Don't you agree?
***Delta**: Yes, I agree.*

Ask questions
Aspen: Do you think that you're being bias against her because she's a woman?

Listen carefully
Delta: *Yes. I guess I am being biased against her. If she wants to have a family, that is none of my concern. The only thing that matters is her ability to do her job competently.*

Mirror response with a You-Statement
Aspen: You are absolutely correct. If she applied for the promotion, then she has the right to get the job if she's the most qualified.

Ask questions
Delta: *So, when should we tell her she got the job?*

Listen carefully
Aspen: Let's do it now!
Delta: *Great, Let's go!*

CALM Dialogue Outcome

By separating gender from the person's qualifications, Delta and Aspin were able to come to an agreement. Robin was the most qualified candidate for the job. Therefore, she got the promotion solely on her qualifications. As well, a win/win outcome was achieved for all. This was because Robin got a much-deserved promotion and the company got the most qualified applicant for the position.

CALM Dialogue Violence Scenario
Scenario Details

Sam and Ash had been friends since college. Sam had majored in Political Science and now worked for the local government. Ash had majored in business and was now employed at a large corporation. Ash had also served in the military for a few years. Ash and Sam both enjoyed hiking. One day while hiking, they had the following conversation.

Conversation begins with an I-Statement
Ash: I'm part of a group that's fighting to take our country back.

Ask questions
Sam*: What group?*

Listen carefully
Ash: It's an underground group. We have discussions in chat rooms about government corruption. In fact, we're planning to gather at the Capital Building next week.

Mirror response with a You-Statement
Sam*: You think the government is corrupt and you're going to peacefully demonstrate outside of the Capital Building? Is that what you're saying?*

Conversation begins with an I-Statement
Ash: I'm not sure if it's going to be peaceful. We want to be heard. We're supposed to bring weapons with us.

Ask questions
Sam*: Wait a minute. Are you going to be participating in a violent act at the Capital Building?*

Listen carefully
Ash: I guess so. I haven't really thought it through.

Mirror response with a You-Statement

***Sam**: You need to think it through. This country was built on peaceful protests and democracy. If you want things to change, you need to do it peacefully. So, if you want to protest, make sure it's done in a nonviolent way without any weapons. Don't you agree?*

Conversation begins with an I-Statement
Ash: Yes, I agree. I do want things to change. However, I don't want to be part of a violent confrontation.

Ask questions
***Sam**: So, I hear you saying that you don't want to be part of the demonstration next week. I think that is a good decision. You can always organize a peaceful protest that does not involve weapons. As well, you can also write letters to your local government officials. There are other ways that your voice can be heard. What do you think?*

Listen carefully
Ash: I agree with you Sam. I think I will make my voice heard in a different way. I'm going to start writing letters to my local officials. I may even run for elected office.

Mirror response with a You-Statement
***Sam**: That's great Ash! I'm so glad we talked.*
Ash: Me too.

CALM Dialogue Outcome

Sometimes just being able to talk about a situation to a neutral person can change the outcome of a potentially violent situation. If Ash hadn't spoken to Sam, Ash wouldn't have realized that there were alternatives to a potentially violent protest. After speaking to Sam, Ash realized there were different ways one could have their voice heard. Therefore, the results of Sam's effective listening skills enabled Ash to visualize an alternative to violence.

Going The Extra Mile

My intention for this chapter is for you to learn how to use the CALM Dialogue. You would need to familiarize yourself with the 4-step process in order to be able to utilize it in your daily life. The key is to use the CALM Dialogue to work through tough issues in a constructive manner. As a result, it will become evident as you become familiar with the process that you will be able to adapt this method to address difficult issues such as race, gender, and violence.

The Wayne Dyer quote at the beginning of the chapter, "It is never crowded along the extra mile," is quite fitting for this section. The fact that you want to learn how to talk about tough issues demonstrates that you are willing to go beyond what is expected of you by others (also known as—going the extra mile). In brief, by acquiring the knowledge along the extra mile—via the CALM Dialogue—you will be able to have difficult conversations that are productive and results focused.

Exercise 1

Write what each letter stands for in the CALM acronym.

C stands for____

A stands for____

L stands for____

M stands for____

Exercise 2

What are some conversations you ***want to have*** using the CALM Dialogue?

1.

2.

3.

4.

5.

6.

7.

8.

9.

10.

Exercise 3

Visualize ***what you will look like*** when you are having a difficult conversation using the CALM Dialogue. You can draw a picture in the box if you want or you can simply visualize it in your mind's eye.

Chapter 7 Word Search

C	T	N	E	M	E	T	A	T	S	E	V	I	T	C	E	L	F	E	R
A	S	O	R	A	T	T	A	B	U	O	G	O	A	Q	O	Y	N	W	E
R	T	N	U	N	D	E	R	S	T	A	N	D	U	N	G	I	E	Y	L
E	A	P	T	T	T	L	I	D	T	E	N	E	E	G	V	L	W	O	F
F	T	L	E	I	B	W	I	B	I	A	S	K	N	D	E	G	O	T	C
U	W	O	U	E	S	L	R	A	R	T	W	R	D	U	R	S	T	S	S
L	R	C	B	A	M	I	H	V	I	N	P	S	E	V	E	T	A	T	T
L	S	T	A	T	E	S	E	O	F	A	W	A	R	E	M	O	I	A	N
Y	Z	O	A	N	C	T	N	A	T	G	R	L	A	M	P	N	R	P	E
D	X	G	S	T	A	S	K	M	E	N	T	O	C	U	A	I	R	Y	M
E	C	U	G	K	F	E	R	H	C	I	A	R	H	H	T	S	O	M	E
D	V	E	H	I	D	F	T	P	H	N	X	U	P	L	H	T	L	E	T
N	B	K	L	K	E	F	Y	E	T	E	B	E	I	J	Y	E	N	N	A
E	N	T	K	Y	M	I	R	R	O	T	X	R	C	I	O	R	O	T	T
N	M	Y	P	A	R	C	O	P	T	S	Y	N	E	C	N	B	V	K	S
E	A	T	D	S	T	Y	T	E	V	I	T	C	E	F	F	E	O	R	U
P	E	L	F	H	E	G	U	Y	A	L	M	O	N	B	O	G	U	E	O
I	S	T	A	T	E	M	E	N	T	S	T	I	O	N	T	E	N	H	Y

Words To Find		
ASK	LISTEN	I STATEMENTS
QUESTIONS	CAREFULLY	YOU STATEMENTS

Chapter 7 Pangram

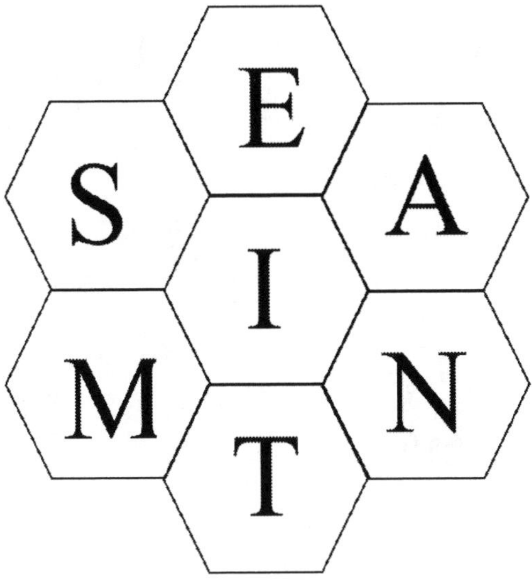

Use all the letters in the pangram to create a word from chapter 7. You can use letters multiple times. Write the word you made below.

____

Chapter 7 Word Scramble

Unscramble the following words.

Scrambled Word	Unscrambled Word
I-matestents	
kas	
notisuesq	
tensil	
cullfeary	
oyu-matestents	

Answers

Chapter 7 Word Search

C	T	N	E	M	E	T	A	T	S	E	V	I	T	C	E	L	F	E	R
A	S	O	R	A	T	T	A	B	U	O	G	O	A	Q	O	Y	N	W	E
R	T	N	U	N	D	E	R	S	T	A	N	D	U	N	G	I	E	Y	L
E	A	P	T	T	T	L	I	D	T	E	N	E	E	G	V	L	W	O	F
F	T	L	E	I	B	W	I	B	I	A	S	K	N	D	E	G	O	T	C
U	W	O	U	E	S	L	R	A	R	T	W	R	D	U	R	S	T	S	S
L	R	C	B	A	M	I	H	V	I	N	P	S	E	V	E	T	A	T	T
L	S	T	A	T	E	S	E	O	F	A	W	A	R	E	M	O	I	A	N
Y	Z	O	A	N	C	T	N	A	T	G	R	L	A	M	P	N	R	P	E
D	X	G	S	T	A	S	K	M	E	N	T	O	C	U	A	I	R	Y	M
E	C	U	G	K	F	E	R	H	C	I	A	R	H	H	T	S	O	M	E
D	V	E	H	I	D	F	T	P	H	N	X	U	P	L	H	T	L	E	T
N	B	K	L	K	E	F	Y	E	T	E	B	E	I	J	Y	E	N	N	A
E	N	T	K	Y	M	I	R	R	O	T	X	R	C	I	O	R	O	T	T
N	M	Y	P	A	R	C	O	P	T	S	Y	N	E	C	N	B	V	K	S
E	A	T	D	S	T	Y	T	E	V	I	T	C	E	F	F	E	O	R	U
P	E	L	F	H	E	G	U	Y	A	L	M	O	N	B	O	G	U	E	O
I	S	T	A	T	E	M	E	N	T	S	T	I	O	N	T	E	N	H	Y

Chapter 7 Pangram Answer

I-Statements

Chapter 7 Word Scramble Answers

Unscrambled Word
I-statements
ask
questions
listen
carefully
you-statements

CHAPTER 8

Dialogue Ignites Change

"Having a mind that is open to everything and attached to nothing seems to me to be one of the most basic principles that you can adopt to contribute to individual and world peace."
-Wayne Dyer

Open-Minded

"Beep, beep, beep" was the sound I heard as the orange light flashed at the luggage carousel. After exiting the plane, I was the first one to arrive at the luggage area to claim my suitcase. I had just gotten divorced and it was the only thing I had left from my old life. It was stuffed with clothes and my two University degrees.

I was filled with hope, anxiety, and fear as I stood in front of the luggage carousel; as I was about to start my new life. Five minutes went by without any sign of my suitcase. Ten minutes went by without any sign of my suitcase. Countless minutes went by without any sign of my suitcase. Suddenly, I was the last person standing in front of the carousel. A few minutes later, the luggage conveyor belt came to a screeching halt.

Panic-stricken and angry, I stood frozen in front of the carousel. Out of nowhere, someone approached me and asked if I needed help. I smiled and said, "My luggage did not arrive." The person then pointed me to the airline's office and told me to go and talk to the airline agents about my suitcase.

The airline agent gave me a stack of forms to fill out. At first, I was overwhelmed with the paperwork, but then I started to relax. I wondered if it would really be a terrible thing if I didn't receive my suitcase. Afterall, I had lost everything else in the divorce, what's one more thing? I also realized that the only thing I didn't lose was my education and knowledge that I had acquired from it. Knowledge was the only thing that I owned at that moment. The paper degrees could always be replaced for a fee, but the knowledge I retained could never be taken away from me.

I then proceeded to fill out the paperwork. When I was finished, I handed it to the agent. She took the papers and looked them over. As I stood there with a new found attitude about my luggage, I heard the office door open. As I looked over to the door, I saw a luggage agent wheeling in a few stray pieces of luggage. To my astonishment, one of them was mine.

In that moment, I felt a sigh of relief. However, I had already made peace with the thought of never seeing my suitcase again. Once I had detached myself from my suitcase, it had managed to appear.

That incident taught me that knowledge is the one thing you can never lose. So, by acquiring knowledge, you will always be able to access it regardless of your location, circumstances, or life situation. Thus, knowledge is intangible and therefore part of your essence and not a physical object. The way I see it, my possessions can be bought, sold, displaced, or lost but my knowledge stays with me wherever I go.

By equipping yourself with the CALM Dialogue, you would be acquiring knowledge about how to constructively engage in difficult conversations. This skill will be one that you can use and carry with you wherever you go. As a result, no one could ever take your knowledge away from you. It is yours to use wherever and however you choose to use it.

The Wayne Dyer quote at the beginning of the chapter is quite fitting for this chapter. As stated by Wayne Dyer, "Having a mind that is open to everything and attached to nothing seems to me to be one of the most basic principles that you can adopt to contribute to individual and world peace." Thus, if you have an open mind about engaging in a difficult conversation, you will be able to take steps towards a more peaceful existence. Once we free ourselves of any negative pre-existing thoughts that prevent us from tackling tough issues, we will be able to move forward into a more accepting and understanding world.

Behavior Reproduction

So, now you have acquired the necessary skills that are required to engage in difficult conversations. You now know the four-step CALM Dialogue, as well as a variety of concepts that will help to guide you along with your constructive conversations.

You are now ready to engage in behavior reproduction in regards to having difficult conversations. As explained by Blanchard and Thacker (2010) "Behavioral reproduction is the transformation of learning into actual behavior" (p. 181). As a matter of fact, you will be engaging in behavioral reproduction via a variety of scenarios that I have created. These scenarios have been inspired by some of the stories I have written about in this book. This will give you a chance to see how a particular situation could have been resolved using the CALM Dialogue. The scenarios are designed to allow you to practice using the CALM Dialogue to guide the conversation along so that they result in a win/win outcome.

Remember that CALM is an acronym. The C stands for—conversation begins with an I-Statement. The A stands for—ask questions. The L stands for—listen carefully. The M stands for—mirror response with a You-Statement. You can use the steps interchangeably, so that the conversation flows naturally. Okay, let's dive into the behavior reproduction scenarios about race, gender, and violence.

Behavior Reproduction Scenario About Race

Scenario Details

This scenario was taken from chapter one. Miss Patel's conversation with Hudson could have gone in a more productive direction if she had been knowledgeable about how to embark on a difficult conversation about race using the CALM Dialogue. Consequently, Miss Patel could have used the conversation as a teachable moment while using the CALM Dialogue process to guide the conversation along.

Hudson was born and raised in Detroit, Michigan. He was a sixteen-year-old African American high school student. He had never traveled outside of the state of Michigan. Additionally, he only had limited interactions with other cultures. He primarily only interacted with different cultures at the high school he attended.

Jennifer Patel was also born and raised in Detroit, Michigan. She was of East Asian descent and grew up in a suburb of Detroit. However, after graduating from teacher's college, she decided to move to the Downtown Detroit area. She didn't really identify with Asians that were born in India because she was raised with American ideals. She was proud to be American.

One day after class, a student named Hudson came to speak to her. They then proceeded to have the following conversation.

Conversation begins with an I-Statement
Hudson: Hey, Miss Patel can I ask you a question?

Ask questions
Miss Patel: *Yes Hudson. What is it?*

Listen carefully
Hudson: Do all East Indian people smell?

Mirror response with a You-Statement
Miss Patel: *No Hudson, that's not true. Do you think I smell?*

Conversation begins with an I-Statement
Hudson: No, I don't think you smell. I can smell your perfume, but other than that, no.

Ask questions
***Miss Patel**: Where did you hear that all East Indian people smell?*

Listen carefully
Hudson: Well, I heard it from my friends. They said that all the East Indian people they've ever been around smell.

Mirror response with a You-Statement
***Miss Patel**: Well, you just said that I don't smell. Therefore, not all East Indian people smell. However, I'm sure there may be a few East Asian people that may smell. But that can be said about any race. You may encounter Caucasians, African Americans, and Native Americans who may smell. However, you shouldn't stereotype all people from a certain race based on a handful of individuals you meet. Do you agree?*

Conversation begins with an I-Statement
Hudson: Yes. I agree. I guess you're right. I just didn't know anyone else who was of East Indian descent to ask.

Conversation begins with an I-Statement
***Miss Patel**: Well, I'm glad that you asked me. That way, I had the opportunity to dispel a terrible stereotype about East Indian people.*

Mirror response with a You-Statement
Hudson: I didn't mean to offend you. I just wanted to talk about it.

Mirror response with a You-Statement
***Miss Patel**: You didn't offend me. I'm glad we talked.*

Conversation begins with an I-Statement
Hudson: I'm glad we talked too.

CALM Dialogue Outcome

Miss Patel was able to separate the individual from the issue in this scenario. She correctly identified Hudson as the individual and the stereotype as the issue. Hudson was simply curious about something he had heard. Thus, by identifying the issue, Miss Patel was able to discuss it constructively with Hudson. This tactic ultimately resulted in a win/win outcome; whereby, Miss Patel was able to squash the stereotype about her race and Hudson was able to discuss the stereotype with her.

Behavior Reproduction Scenario About Gender

Scenario Details

This scenario was taken from chapter four. In my mind, this is how a conversation between Mila and her mother—Astrid— could have gone after she had encountered her ex-husband Jake at the grocery store. By utilizing the four-step CALM Dialogue process, Mila could have addressed the double standards in regards to gender that had plagued her life.

Mila was a woman in her forties. She had received her MBA (Master of Business Administration) in her twenties. She became an accountant and had a good career. She was able to travel and enjoy the fruits of her labor. In her thirties, she got married to Jake. Mila then moved abroad with Jake for his career. They tried to have children but were not able to conceive, even with the help of fertility treatments. They later returned back to their home country. Shortly after their return home, they divorced. A year after their divorce, Mila ran in to Jake at the grocery store. She discovered that he had a child and was not remarried. She was taken aback by the realization that if she had a child out of wedlock, she would be stigmatized by her family and community. Mila was upset about the double standards that plagued her simply because she was a woman.

Astrid was Mila's mother. She was a devout Christian and had grown up in the church. However, she had also gotten divorced from her abusive, alcoholic husband. Even though it was the best thing for her and Mila, she was inadvertently stigmatized by church members. That was why she was always so hard on Mila. She wanted Mila to be perfect, so that everyone could see that her divorce was the best thing for both of them. Astrid was desperate for the approval of her church members. So, she made sure that Mila did everything right according to her judgmental church friends. Astrid was devastated when Mila announced her divorce. Now, she felt like she was a failure in the eyes of the community. However, she knew that Mila was a wonderful daughter and she was very proud of her; she just didn't know how to express it.

After Mila encountered Jake at the grocery, she went home and had the following conversation with her mother, Astrid. Before she began speaking, she did the Dandelion relaxation exercise to settle her nerves.

Conversation begins with an I-Statement
Mila: I just ran in to Jake at the grocery store.

Ask questions
Astrid: *How's he doing?*

Listen carefully
Mila: He had a baby with him. He has had a son since we divorced and he's not remarried.

Mirror response with a You-Statement
Astrid: *Are you serious? I had no idea he had a son.*

Conversation begins with an I-Statement
Mila: I'm as serious as a heart attack.

Ask questions
Mila: Why is that okay? Why can he have a child out of wedlock and no one seems to care? Whereas, if it were me, the whole country would've called you to tell you how shameful it was for me to have a child out of wedlock!

Listen carefully
Astrid: *I understand you are frustrated. You know that the church people mean well. I know that it sounds hypocritical, however, that's how it is.*

Mirror response with a You-Statement
Mila: Why are you protecting them. They're so judgmental and hypocritical. Why do you care what they think?

Conversation begins with an I-Statement
Astrid: *I don't know why I care. I guess I just want to fit in. I want to belong to a group.*

Ask questions
Mila: At what cost? They make your life miserable. All they do is sit around and judge everyone.

Listen carefully
***Astrid**: You're right Mila. We've lived our lives to please people who really don't care about us. You're also right about the fact that they're hypocrites.*

Mirror response with a You-Statement
Mila: I'm glad that you've finally seen the light. After all this time, you can finally see that they don't care about us.

Conversation begins with an I-Statement
***Astrid**: I'm sorry about being so judgmental about your life, Mila. I should have not been so hard on you.*

Ask questions
Mila: Are you really sorry?

Listen carefully
***Astrid**: Yes, I am. I just want you to be happy. From now on, go and live your life with no regrets. You're still young. You have a long life ahead of you.*

Mirror response with a You-Statement
Mila: Thank you, mom. I love you.

Mirror response with a You-Statement
***Astrid**: I love you too, Mila.*

CALM Dialogue Outcome

Astrid was finally able to focus on the big picture. She realized that Mila still had a long life ahead of her, and therefore, it was time for them to move forward in their lives without judgement. By encouraging Mila to focus on her future and live without regrets, they will be able to move beyond their past relationship that was plagued with gender bias. By the end of their conversation, Mila and Astrid had arrived at a win/win outcome. Mila was able to move forward and live her life as she saw fit, and Astrid was able to let go of her judgement and maintain a good relationship with her daughter.

Behavior Reproduction Scenario About Violence

Scenario Details

This scenario was taken from chapter four. For me, the scenario could have ended differently if either Chloe or Clayton were knowledgeable about how to have difficult conversations using the CALM Dialogue. By utilizing the CALM Dialogue instead of a baseball bat, Chloe could have refrained from violence and may have even changed the course of her future with Clayton. As well, Clayton could have handled the situation better. Instead of breaking up with her over the phone, he could have talked to her in person using the four-step process. All in all, instead of walking away from the situation with a lose/lose outcome—perhaps they would have walked away with a win/win outcome.

Chloe was in her twenties. She had been dating Clayton for a few years. Her family and friends loved him. Clayton had even been on vacation with them. Chloe was close with her family and desperately sought their approval about everything. That's why she was thrilled that they embraced Clayton. Chloe was hoping to get engaged soon. Marriage was important to her because her parents had been married for decades and seemed to be happy.

Clayton was in his twenties as well. He had been dating Chloe for a few years, and he got along well with her family. Clayton loved Chloe, but did not like her temper. He found her to be a bit too dramatic at times. As well, he was getting a bit anxious because she was always bringing up the topic of marriage. However, he wasn't ready for marriage as yet. In fact, he was actually scared of marriage. This is because he remembers how messy his parents' divorce was. He had recently reconnected with his ex-girlfriend. He had met her at a restaurant because she was in town visiting some relatives. It was easy to talk to her because there was no pressure of a romantic relationship looming over his head. They talked and laughed and had a good visit.

The day after he had met his ex-girlfriend for dinner, Chloe called him in a rage. She had heard that he had dinner with his other girlfriend. Instead of clarifying the story, Clayton simply agreed with her. He was tired of her always getting angry at any little thing. He then proceeded to tell her that they should take a break from the relationship for a while. After he hung up the phone, he immediately realized that he did not handle the situation well. Clayton then picked the phone up and called Chloe back. He told her that he wanted to discuss this situation in person. He then asked her if he could come over and speak with her. She told him that she would rather them talk at his place. He agreed and Chloe drove over to Clayton's house and they had the following conversation.

Conversation begins with an I-Statement
Clayton: I wanted to talk to you about everything in person.

Ask questions
***Chloe**: What do you have to say?*

Listen carefully
Clayton: Chloe, I don't have another girlfriend. I just saw my ex-girlfriend because she was in town and wanted to tell me that she was getting married.

Mirror response with a You-Statement
***Chloe**: So, you don't have another girlfriend? Why did you say you did then?*

Conversation begins with an I-Statement
Clayton: I just wanted you to stop yelling.

Ask questions
***Chloe**: Do you still want to break up?*

Listen carefully
Clayton: I don't know. I'm a little nervous about moving forward and getting married. My parents had a really messy divorce a few years ago. So, it messed me up.

Mirror response with a You-Statement
***Chloe**: You are a bit hesitant about marriage. I get that. I'm glad that I came over to talk.*

Conversation begins with an I-Statement
Clayton: I'm glad you came over too. I just need to figure things out. That's maybe why I said we need to take a break. It's to make sure that I can sort my thoughts out.

Ask questions
Chloe*: Have you thought about going to see a therapist or counselor about it?*

Listen carefully
Clayton: Yes. I've been thinking about it. I've even looked a few up online.

Mirror response with a You-Statement
Chloe*: You should give them a call; I think it's a good idea. I think you're doing the right thing. Everyone should be certain if marriage is right for them before they do it. It's a huge step.*

Conversation begins with an I-Statement
Clayton: I'm glad that you understand. I didn't mean to hurt you.

Mirror response with a You-Statement
Chloe*: I know you didn't mean to hurt me.*

Listen carefully
Chloe*: I think I should get therapy too. I get very angry about things. In fact, I even thought about breaking up your red sports car with a bat. How foolish was that?*

Mirror response with a You-Statement
Clayton: You did? I'm glad that you didn't do that.

Conversation begins with an I-Statement
Chloe*: I'm glad that I didn't let my rage consume me. I'm glad that we talked.*

Listen carefully
Clayton: Maybe we should both book appointments with therapists tomorrow. That way we can both work on our issues before we move forward in our relationship.

Mirror response with a You-Statement
Chloe*: I agree. I'll text you tomorrow.*

Conversation begins with an I-Statement
Clayton: I'm glad we talked. I feel better.

Conversation begins with an I-Statement
Chloe: *I feel better too. Good night.*

CALM Dialogue Outcome

Clayton was driven by his internal locus of control to have a difficult conversation with Chloe about their relationship. He was able to reframe the conversation he had initially had on the phone in order to clarify the break-up and dinner with his ex-girlfriend. As a result, Chloe and Clayton were able to focus on the bigger picture—which revolved around marriage. By focusing on the big picture, they both agreed that they each needed counseling before they could move forward with their relationship. Chloe agreed to seek counseling for her anger; which was something that was a concern for Clayton. As well, Clayton agreed to seek counseling for his commitment issues; which was something that concerned Chloe. In the end, the decision to seek counseling resulted in a win/win outcome for them both. Whereas, if the situation had been handled differently (as it was in chapter four), it would have resulted in a lose/lose outcome that would have led to a violent attack on Clayton's red sports car and the end of their relationship forever.

My Intention

My intention for this chapter is for you to utilize the behavior reproduction scenarios to hone your dialogical skills. It is my hope that once you become comfortable using the CALM Dialogue—by practicing it through these exercises—you will be ready to use it in your life. Additionally, you can create your own scenarios using the CALM Dialogue Templates contained in the Appendix section at the end of this book. Thus, by practicing using the CALM Dialogue, you will be prepared to engage in conversations about difficult topics such as race, gender, and violence.

We have now come to the end of my teaching. This brings to mind a scene from *The Matrix* when Morpheus says to Neo, "I can only show you the door. You are the one who has to walk through it." Similarly, I too have shown you the door to embarking on difficult conversations. Now, you must walk through it—by using the knowledge you have acquired to tackle the tough issues in your life.

Dialogue ignites change! I absolutely believe that this statement is true. Therefore, by using the framework laid out for you in this book, I believe that tough issues can be discussed in order to bring about change in our relationships, our communities, and our world. For we create our reality with our thoughts, actions, and words.

Exercise 1

Circle all the phrases that you think apply to you.

I am a people pleaser	I do not need to please others
I am a good listener	I do not listen to others well
I talk over others	I give others the opportunity to speak
I see things the way others see things	I see things differently from others
I am empathetic	I do not feel empathy for others
I am aware of things that bother me	I am not aware of things that bother me
I think before I speak	I say the first thing that comes to mind
I take charge of my life	I let life happen

You can compare your answers to your answers in chapter one.
Did any of your answers change?

Exercise 2

List the Names of people that ***you are going to share*** the CALM Dialogue process with.

1.

2.

3.

4.

5.

6.

7.

8.

9.

10.

11.

12.

13.

14.

15.

16.

17.

18.

19.

20.

Exercise 3

Visualize ***what you look like*** when you are faced with conflict. You can draw a picture in the box if you want or you can simply visualize it in your mind's eye.

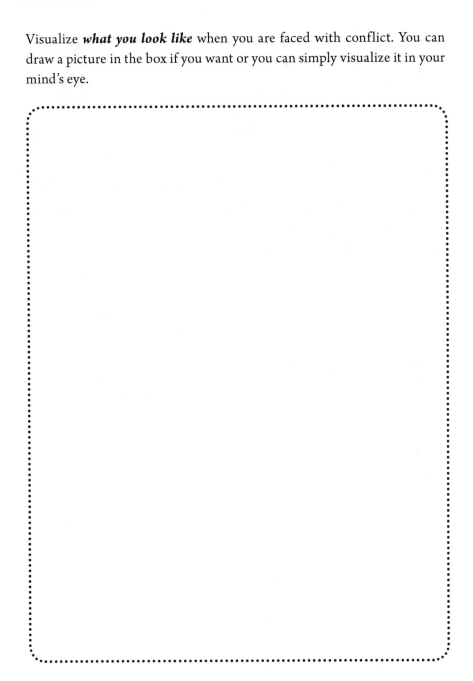

Compare your picture to the exercise in chapter one. Did your picture change?

Chapter 8 Word Search

P A C G E N T P M A O G N I M A R F E R
A Y O R A T T A B U O G F A B O E N O O
T T G A Y T I V I T I S O P I N L M Y L
E A F M T T L I D T E N V E T V A W O E
P T B E A B W I B I W T E N D U X O T P
D W I U E L L R A R I W R D N R A T S I
E R G B G N I W N I W P S I V S T E T N
S S P A T E S O N T R O M U H A I I A D
U Z I A N C T E N T I A L A M V O R P I
C X C S T A S K M E T T O C U I N R Y V
O C T G K F E R H I F A R H H O S O M I
F V U H I D F T O H L F U P L L T L E D
E B R L N O I T P E C R E P J E E N N U
R N E K Y M I R R O R X R C I N R O T A
U M Y P E R C E P T I O N E T C B V K L
T A T D S T Y T E M E N T S I E W O R P
U E N O I S S U E S I D I A B O G U E S
F F R T E D L O R T N O C F O S U C O L

Words To Find			
INDIVIDUAL	REFRAMING	PYGMALION EFFECT	LOCUS OF CONTROL
ISSUE	PERCEPTION	RELAXATION	FUTURE FOCUSED
HUMOR	WIN WIN	POSITIVITY	BIG PICTURE

Chapter 8 Pangram

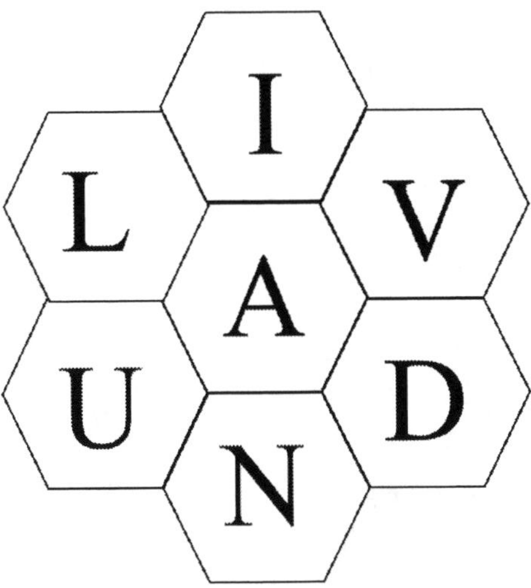

Use all the letters in the pangram to create a word from chapter 8. You can use letters multiple times. Write the word you made below.

Chapter 8 Word Scramble

Unscramble the following words.

Scrambled Word	Unscrambled Word
dividinlua	
receptionp	
niwinw	
cuslo fo trolcon	
sitpotviyi	
turfue suedfoc	
sueis	
rumho	
gib ripecut	
minefargr	
galionmyp teefcf	
lionrextaa	

Answers

Chapter 8 Word Search

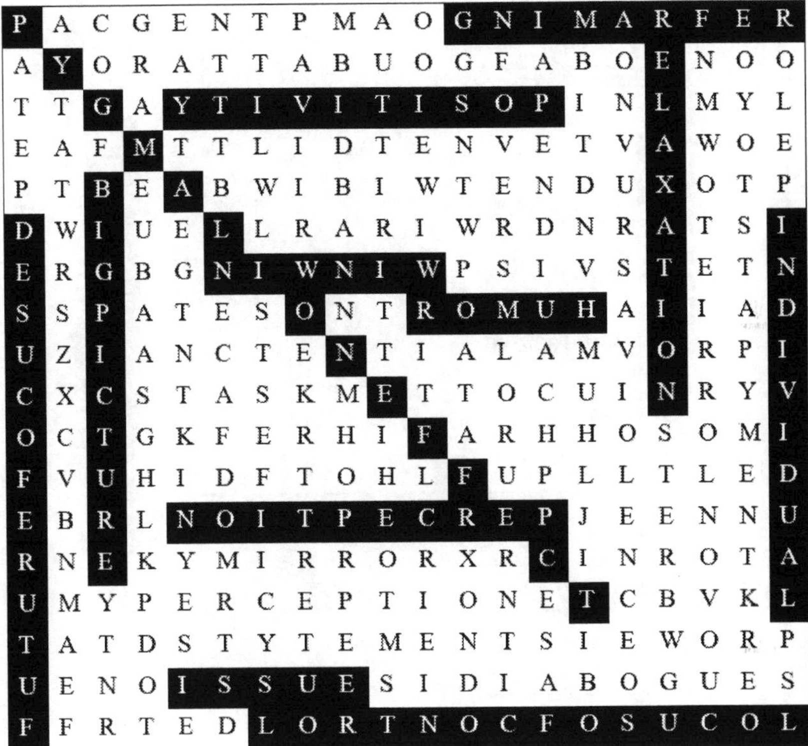

Chapter 8 Pangram Answer

Individual

Chapter 8 Word Scramble Answers

Unscrambled Word
individual
perception
win win
locus of control
positivity
future focused
issue
humor
big picture
reframing
pygmalion effect
relaxation

REFERENCES

Adler, N. J. (2008). *International Dimensions of Organizational Behavior* (5th ed.). Cengage Learning.

Blanchard, P. N., & Thacker, J. W. (2010). *Effective Training: Systems, Strategies, and Practices* (4th ed.). Pearson.

Covey, S. (2004). *The 7 Habits of Highly Effective People.* Simon & Schuster.

Dubrin, A. (2013). *Leadership: Research Findings, Practice, and Skills* (7th ed.). Cengage Learning.

Fisher, R., Ury, W., & Patton, B. (2011). *Getting to Yes* (3rd ed.). Penguin Books.

Kreitner, R., & Kinicki, A. (2013). *Organizational Behavior* (10th ed.). McGraw-Hill/Irwin.

Lussier, R. N., & Achua, C. F. (2016). *Leadership: Theory, Application, & Skill Development* (6th ed.). Cengage Learning.

Merriam, S. B., & Bierema, L. L. (2014). *Adult Learning.* Jossey-Bass.

APPENDIX

CALM Dialogue Practice Scenario About Race

Scenario Details

Conversation begins with an I-Statement

Ask questions

Listen carefully

Mirror response with a You-Statement

Conversation begins with an I-Statement

Ask questions

Listen carefully

Mirror response with a You-Statement

Conversation begins with an I-Statement

Ask questions

Listen carefully

Mirror response with a You-Statement

Conversation begins with an I-Statement

Ask questions

Listen carefully

Mirror response with a You-Statement

Conversation begins with an I-Statement

Ask questions

Listen carefully

Mirror response with a You-Statement

Conversation begins with an I-Statement

Ask questions

Listen carefully

Mirror response with a You-Statement

Conversation begins with an I-Statement

Ask questions

Listen carefully

Mirror response with a You-Statement

Conversation begins with an I-Statement

Ask questions

Listen carefully

Mirror response with a You-Statement

Conversation begins with an I-Statement

Ask questions

Listen carefully

Mirror response with a You-Statement

CALM Dialogue Outcome

CALM Dialogue Practice Scenario About Gender

Scenario Details

Conversation begins with an I-Statement

Ask questions

Listen carefully

Mirror response with a You-Statement

Conversation begins with an I-Statement

Ask questions

Listen carefully

Mirror response with a You-Statement

Conversation begins with an I-Statement

Ask questions

Listen carefully

Mirror response with a You-Statement

Conversation begins with an I-Statement

Ask questions

Listen carefully

Mirror response with a You-Statement

Conversation begins with an I-Statement

Ask questions

Listen carefully

Mirror response with a You-Statement

Conversation begins with an I-Statement

Ask questions

Listen carefully

Mirror response with a You-Statement

Conversation begins with an I-Statement

Ask questions

Listen carefully

Mirror response with a You-Statement

Conversation begins with an I-Statement

Ask questions

Listen carefully

Mirror response with a You-Statement

Conversation begins with an I-Statement

Ask questions

Listen carefully

Mirror response with a You-Statement

CALM Dialogue Outcome

CALM Dialogue Practice Scenario About Violence

Scenario Details

Conversation begins with an I-Statement

Ask questions

Listen carefully

Mirror response with a You-Statement

Conversation begins with an I-Statement

Ask questions

Listen carefully

Mirror response with a You-Statement

Conversation begins with an I-Statement

Ask questions

Listen carefully

Mirror response with a You-Statement

Conversation begins with an I-Statement

Ask questions

Listen carefully

Mirror response with a You-Statement

Conversation begins with an I-Statement

Ask questions

Listen carefully

Mirror response with a You-Statement

Conversation begins with an I-Statement

Ask questions

Listen carefully

Mirror response with a You-Statement

Conversation begins with an I-Statement

Ask questions

Listen carefully

Mirror response with a You-Statement

Conversation begins with an I-Statement

Ask questions

Listen carefully

Mirror response with a You-Statement

Conversation begins with an I-Statement

Ask questions

Listen carefully

Mirror response with a You-Statement

CALM Dialogue Outcome

CALMDialoguePracticeScenarioAbout___________________________

Scenario Details

Conversation begins with an I-Statement

Ask questions

Listen carefully

Mirror response with a You-Statement

Conversation begins with an I-Statement

Ask questions

Listen carefully

Mirror response with a You-Statement

Conversation begins with an I-Statement

Ask questions

Listen carefully

Mirror response with a You-Statement

Conversation begins with an I-Statement

Ask questions

Listen carefully

Mirror response with a You-Statement

Conversation begins with an I-Statement

Ask questions

Listen carefully

Mirror response with a You-Statement

Conversation begins with an I-Statement

Ask questions

Listen carefully

Mirror response with a You-Statement

Conversation begins with an I-Statement

Ask questions

Listen carefully

Mirror response with a You-Statement

Conversation begins with an I-Statement

Ask questions

Listen carefully

Mirror response with a You-Statement

Conversation begins with an I-Statement

Ask questions

Listen carefully

Mirror response with a You-Statement

CALM Dialogue Outcome

ABOUT THE AUTHOR

Joy Rich's academic achievements include an MBA, LL.B. (Law Degree), and a B.A. in Political Science. She was also a Florida Supreme Court Certified Family Mediator. Additionally, she is a skilled ADR trainer. Joy has taught thousands of people the CALM Dialogue; a 4-Step conflict resolution method she developed. The primary focus of her attention is now on creating peaceful resolution techniques that will aid in the advancement of communication for all.

Printed in the United States
by Baker & Taylor Publisher Services